THE
Cactus of Sanity

By

Sergey Baranov

Copyright 2020 Sergey Baranov. All rights reserved.

No part of this book may be reproduced in any form without written permission from the author.

This book should not be construed as encouraging the illegal use of psychedelic substances and plants outside of a guided shamanic ceremony or a country where this is permitted by law. Neither the author nor the publisher are responsible for any possible legal, physical, psychological, and/or other consequences if the reader chooses to ignore this warning.

Editor — Dereck Daschke

Drawings — Francisco Javier Ruiz Nuñez

Dedicated to my dear, beautiful, loving and beloved wife Mercedes.

ACKNOWLEDGEMENTS

My deep and sincere gratitude to all the forces that have been guiding and protecting me on my path and finally bringing me home to the Sacred Valley of the Incas, Peru, where, together with my family, we live, love and learn under the tutelage of the sacred Huachuma cactus.

Huachuma makes us see the world of inescapable beauty, to which we naturally react with love. This love is the spirit healer. A book is a snapshot of an author in time. It is me today. It is what I think and believe to be true. I measure my writing by the sincerity of my feelings, not word count. Its depth, if any, is for you to judge.

It is my hope that this book will serve you as a light dose of my medicine that will help you maintain your sanity during this time of chaos and beyond.

Escaping false beliefs is one of the many self-imposed tasks I have managed to achieve over the years of spiritual searching. What I present here is a result of this journey. Huachuma is a wise and loving plant-teacher, whose experience cannot be disproved. It is unique, self-evident and revealing.

A view of the Apu Pitusiray from Huachuma Wasi

www.huachumawasi.com

HUACHUMAN

Table of Contents

Editorial Reviews 1

Foreword 4

Introduction 7

Part I : Shamanic Healing In My Life And Work 18

   Chapter 1 : 2020, The Year Of Chaos And Great Opportunity 19

   Chapter 2 : The Shamanic Bridge To A Better Future ... 39

   Chapter 3 : Envisioning Your Life 51

   Chapter 4 : The Source Of Inner Peace 58

   Chapter 5 : I Want To Be Me 66

   Chapter 6 : Objective Reality Of The Heart 77

   Chapter 7 : Meeting Patrick Swayze In The Bathroom: Hollywood Encounters Huachuma 84

Part II : The Cactus Of Sanity 95

   Chapter 8 : Huachuma, The Healing Visionary Cactus From Peru 96

   Chapter 9 : Huachuma's Place In History 106

   Chapter 10 : Huachuma, The Unforgettable Mystery .. 114

Chapter 11 : The Healing Beauty Of Huachuma..........122

Chapter 12 : Huachuma Is The Liquid Sun.................128

Chapter 13 : Huachuma And The Third Eye...............140

Chapter 14 : Huachuma, The House Built On The Rock 150

Chapter 15 : Huachuma And The Meaning Of Life 153

Part III : Diagnosing The Modern World 163

Chapter 16 : Consciousness In Exile: A Shamanic Perspective 164

Chapter 17 : Militarized Psychiatry Vs. Plant Medicine 174

Chapter 18 : The Essence Of Huachuma Cactus 192

Chapter 19 : The Convenience Of A City Is Inconvenient To Your Soul 195

Chapter 20 : Individuality Vs. The Collective.............210

Chapter 21 : Self-Consuming Consumerism................223

Chapter 22 : Huachuma Cactus Vs. Techno-Idolatry ..233

Chapter 23 : A.I. And The Synthetic Reality: Horrors And Hopes For The Future 245

Chapter 24 : On Mind...255

Chapter 25 : Who Is Richard Dawkins For Richard Dawkins? 267

Chapter 26 : The Elephant In The Room 280

Epilogue Cusco, Where Ancient History Keeps Coming Back With More 322

EDITORIAL REVIEWS

"The Cactus of Sanity is a heart-felt report from a dedicated student of plant medicines. This is the third book in a series by Sergey Baranov and it focuses on his relationship with Huachuma, San Pedro. Baranov describes a life-long yearning for a direct experience of the mystical realms - "Plant teachers are the gateway to the World of Spirits where healing and guidance are found." Read this book for an intimate description of how a life can be transformed in service of plant medicines."

-Rachel Harris, PhD
Listening to Ayahuasca: New Hope for Depression, Addiction, PTSD, and Anxiety

"The Cactus of Sanity: Huachuma in a Time of Chaos unfolds for the reader much like a ceremony with this light-filled plant itself, the luminous text filling the reader's mind with liberating ideas and an endless stream of insights gleaned from the author's deep mystical experiences in various locations in and around Peru's Sacred Valley, the famous "Eagle's Nest" — a 3,000-year-old location high in the snow-capped Andes mountains where Huachuma (also called San Pedro cactus) was consumed reverentially. The author also treats us to accounts of visiting sacred locations like the Chavin and other sites where this entheogen leads him into altered states and profound connections to nature and his deepest infinite self — a self of blinding white light that will be familiar to high-level yogis and students of nondual philosophy and practice.

The author — Sergey Baranov — includes rich biographical details of his intuitive journey from his birthplace in Russia and childhood in Israel to his experiences living in a cult in Northern California, and the magical signs and messages that eventually called him to Peru where he trained as a curandero in the local traditions there and — after the medicine opened his own heart — led him to opening the hearts of others with this unique plant that's sacred to the Quecha-speaking people.

The book arrives in the midst of what feels like the beginning of a Kali Yuga or time of chaos, and offers very compelling arguments that Huachuma and its cousins in the kingdom of psychedelic plants are perhaps the best accelerators of a higher consciousness desperately needed as the World Economic Forum, the U.N., and an alphabet soup of international agencies and central banks installing an AI control system in what some call the rise of the bio-security state, which — being a creature of eugenicists and technocrats — allows no space for spirituality or true human freedom.

From this vantage point, Baranov's book may be the much-needed medicine industrial society needs as it circles a

The Cactus of Sanity

technological abyss about which Orwell and Huxley warned us decades ago."

-Guy Crittenden is a journalist and author of *The Year of Drinking Magic: Twelve Ceremonies with the Vine of Souls* (Apocryphile Press, San Francisco) which won the Silver Medal at the 2018 Independent Book Publisher Awards. Crittenden lives in Innisfil, Ontario, Canada and many of his writings can be found on his website HipGnosis.co

"Sergey Baranov's latest book shows you, via teachings of San Pedro (Huachuma), how it is essential to unlearn the past and allow the medicine to reprogram your neural pathways so you can relearn and awaken to this new World. Psychotropic medicine plants bring us neurogenesis and neuroplasticity, rewiring neural connections that we have been programmed with since birth. These things can be reprogrammed with the master plants. In this book, Sergey shows you the way to do this. There are times when you think you should do something and there are times when you are definitely called to do something. Sergey was called to follow the path of healing via Huachuma medicine. His story will lead you, if you ever had any questions. A must-read!"

-Alan Shoemaker, author of *Ayahuasca Medicine*

FOREWORD

All those who feel drawn to the spiritual quest can rejoice that Sergey Baranov has produced yet another book. As the subtitle suggests, this book could not be more timely. Indeed, this year of 2020 is definitely a time of chaos. We have a global pandemic to cope with, democracies on the edge of collapse, climate change is upon us in a way that can't be denied, rioting in the streets demanding racial and social justice, and more. The immediate future looks bad. Very, very bad. On the collective level, we need leadership with vision. On a personal level we each need inner guidance to align ourselves with the deepest truths and to throw off, rise above the egoic habits and blinders that keep us stuck in the current reality.

Baranov is all about personal, mystical vision. In this book, he's deeply distrustful of rationalism, science, and traditional religion. Ever since he was five years of age, he tells us, he felt drawn to spirit, questioning the societal givens. He found that neither science nor reason could provide the answers we need for survival. It's been a quest for meaning. Why are we here? What's our true nature? Where are we going?

The Cactus of Sanity

Baranov has found the guidance he was seeking all his life in "Huachuma," which refers to the San Pedro cactus that's abundant in the Andean valley in Peru where he lives and conducts retreats, while tapping into the timeless shamanic knowledge and ceremonies surrounding plant medicine. He does not claim to be a shaman; rather, he is a humble guide to visionary experience through his writing and retreats.

Key autobiographical details of his own journey are scattered throughout the book along with discussions summarizing the theories of major figures from the various camps of rationality as well as those who have found rationality to be too limiting. For example, he writes: "Neither religion nor science have emphasized the importance of the visionary experiences that have preceded both [science and religion]."

Especially telling is the following passage, "The point I'm trying to get across is that reason is just a tool, a useful tool to go by in worldly affairs but limited in application to Divine matters. We can call it the unconscious mind, the Other, an inspiration, a sign, a Daemon voice, or any other name. There is something beyond what a rational mind can grasp that keeps guiding and inspiring many people through history, something that science calls delusional, delirious and hallucinatory, while religion refers to it as demonic. We can debate its origin, whether it is our unconscious mind or an outside force, but the facts of its existence are, to me, doubtless and beyond all debate."

This latest book from Sergey Baranov is timely, well-written, and inspiring.

David Van Nuys, PhD.
Emeritus Prof. of Psychology
Host: ShrinkRapRadio.com

INTRODUCTION

"The intuitive mind is a sacred gift and the rational mind is a faithful servant. We have created a society that honors the servant and has forgotten the gift."

— Albert Einstein

Peru is still under lockdown as I finish writing this book. Looking through my window, I see beautiful, peaceful mountains that stand still. When I cooked medicine in February, I had a feeling that this medicine would not be used this year. It was a strange feeling. Why wouldn't it be? I was expecting many people who had already booked their flights and many others who had contacted me and expressed their intention to come. But the feeling was clear. It will be a while before the medicine I prepared in February will be used. I was puzzled. Two weeks after I finished cooking, on March 16, 2020, the Peruvian government announced the lockdown.

Empty streets, everything is closed. Everyday feels like Sunday. I lost track of days, weeks and, now, months. I had to cancel making a new documentary at the sacred sites of Lake Titicaca, where I planned to go at the end of April. My intention was to follow the vision I had last time I visited the lake, to take people on a Huachuma journey at the ancient sacred places and film it all in real time. After this, I was planning to make a few more documentaries this year, taking people to the most ancient and powerful places of Peru. We call them Huacas, sacred sites. All plans are cancelled. On a positive note, our family has now made an even stronger bond. We always have been a medicine to one another, and today we are even more. Together we surf the waves of global madness in a boat of love.

Those who have set up their life in connection with Nature are feeling the negative effects of the mass psychoses to a much lesser degree, if any. I write these words during the peak of the coronavirus hysteria. I am in my center, I am in my strength. I am not afraid, and I can see it for what it is. I feel sorry for my children, that they cannot go outside to play, ride a bicycle, take dancing classes or go to school to meet with their friends. I feel sorry for people who were unprepared and now are suffering a great deal. But I can see through it like through a window. It's just another test for who we are and what we stand for, for our love for one another, for our life vision. Can we hold on to it in the midst of the chaos? Or, like dust, will we be blown away by the fear?

I cannot express my gratitude enough to Huachuma medicine for what it did to my heart, mind and spirit over many years of working with it. The established connection with my own self is what serves me, my family and my friends as a shelter against the hurricane of confusion and fear we see in the world today. Like a cactus, I stand still in the midst of mass psychoses.

Sergey Baranov

I took a "therapeutic" (micro-) dose of Huachuma today to outline the vision for this book. I write these words as a surge of warm feeling comes through me. For nearly five weeks I was consumed by the news, like a forest is consumed by a wildfire. I became extremely active on social media, burning my precious time in mindless arguments with people who seemed to choose denialism as their way to defend themselves from the inconvenient truth. These kinds of arguments are the most depleting. It feels like you are talking to a wall: an utter waste of time and energy.

I felt that, in order to break this destructive trend, I had to give myself a new task: to write another book. This will be the first book I have written under the stress of the new political environment. The first two, *PATH: Seeking Truth in a World of Lies*,[1] published in 2013, and the latest, *The Mescaline Confession: Breaking through the World of Delusion*,[2] published in 2018, were both written feeling the urgency of the expected worldly chaos. When I wrote my first book, I felt there was still time for the world to come to its senses. Writing my second book was more of a warning of an impending social calamity. But this book has been written during the most stressful time our world has seen since the Second World War, and even then places like South America were distant from it and people lived normal lives. Today, South America is on lockdown, moving through the madness like everyone else. All countries and everyone's lives are affected.

Anyhow, we continue living our lives under new conditions. We nurture one another with love, and Huachuma keeps us sane. The quarantine affects our roads and our livelihood but not our hearts, minds and spirit. Today, I sacrifice nothing to have everything. I live the best life I can. Fulfilled and content, I'm here to serve Huachuma until my last breath. If I got a chance to change anything in my life, I would refuse it. All the suffering I had to endure made me what I am today. I am nothing without my past. My past is my spiritual parent; my demons became my friends, my pain led me to find my joy.

Not only do I write this book as a way to use the quarantine time wisely but also to provide support to all my friends, guests, and people I will meet in the future, and even those whose paths I will never cross. It is my hope you find this book useful and share it with others you think it could help as well.

In my previous books I've shared my path and my work with Ayahuasca and Peyote, each powerful plant teachers that helped me on my path. I respect both and recommend you work with them in the right way and with the right people. But for whatever reason, I was called to serve Huachuma as my main teacher and guide in this life. I wish I could just use words to make you feel the love and the beauty of this amazing, ancient plant teacher and healer. But this is just as impossible as conveying the scent of Huachuma flowers with words. It is something you have to experience to know.

The Cactus of Sanity

My life was transformed on this path and became more than I wished for. I found my family walking this path, built a nest for it and keep serving it with all the love I can find in my heart. Together my wife and I built Huachuma Wasi, the "Cactus House" in the native Quechua language of the Andes, to share our way of life with people who are seeking answers. If I can do more with my life, it will be great. If not, what I have already done is enough to live in peace.

For many years I was telling people that by going back, we are moving forward. What I meant is that by going back in history and reviving the ancient shamanic traditions, we find the connection with ourselves and Nature that hold the keys for healing and spiritual growth. A healthy way forward has to be based on real connection. The particular grounding found in Huachuma is essential for living one's life. It is a dose of sanity that heals with love, the self-evident truth that comes in the form of understanding. It removes self-doubts, fears and despair. Huachuma helps you to reignite the flame that burned in you when you were a happy child living in a world of wonder. It is magic. It is something that can be only felt.

When I finished writing *The Mescaline Confession*, I saw what was coming to our world. The medicine was showing me this in sometimes painful detail. Here is the final paragraph of that book:

"As the world is going mad, your health, your sanity, and your connection to yourself must become your greatest assets. There is no time to be wasted on false fears and stereotypes surrounding plant medicine. For our stuck-in-your-head culture, plant medicine shamanism is the way out from the labyrinths of the mind and is a direct path to self-knowledge and well-being. Huachuma Wasi provides a platform for healing and spiritual growth. Come to visit, stay, and share with us a profound shamanic experience facilitated in a passionate and loving way. Be our guest and let us learn from you as you learn from us. You too can bloom!"

Two years later, this paragraph is even more relevant than it was when I wrote it. Today, looking forward, I can see a greater need for plant medicine connection in our lives as we have entered the cycle of confusion and turbulence, moving through which will decide our fate. Love is the best medicine known to man. But sometimes, in order to reach for it, we have to pull off the layers of fear. Huachuma gives you the hand to take you gently through it.

The Cactus of Sanity

I think that final paragraph of my previous book can be continued as follows:

If you think that keeping a certain diet puts you on a pedestal and makes you spiritual, you are mistaken. If you think that holding hands and singing mantras gives you higher moral ground and makes you spiritual, you are mistaken. If you think that playing a guitar and serving medicine makes you spiritual, you are mistaken. These are only attributes of a spiritual lifestyle that may or may not result in a kind of Self you are trying to create by following different disciplines and healing modalities. One can have an appearance of wisdom and yet remain shallow inside. Your true spirituality is what you stand for, your system of values that you based your life on. What makes you spiritual is your love of freedom. What makes you spiritual are your efforts to make our world a better place for all. It's not how you look or sing, it's how you feel and think about life that matters. At least for me.

The time we have entered is a time of chaos and truth that will shatter all bubbles and tear away all mental masks. It's the time to test who we are and what we stand for. No one will be able to hide in one's little world. The reality is reaching down to everyone, regardless of how thick the walls you have built around your mind. The current world situation is just the first wave. More waves will follow to rock your boat. Denialism is no longer a safe shelter where you can hide from reality. In fact, it will catch up with you at the most unexpected moment.

To each his own, of course, and if my words do not make sense to you, that is fine with me. You can hate me for what I say, but you can also use my words as a mirror that shows you where you stand in your worldview and let you move in a better direction, using it as a reference point. The choice is yours.

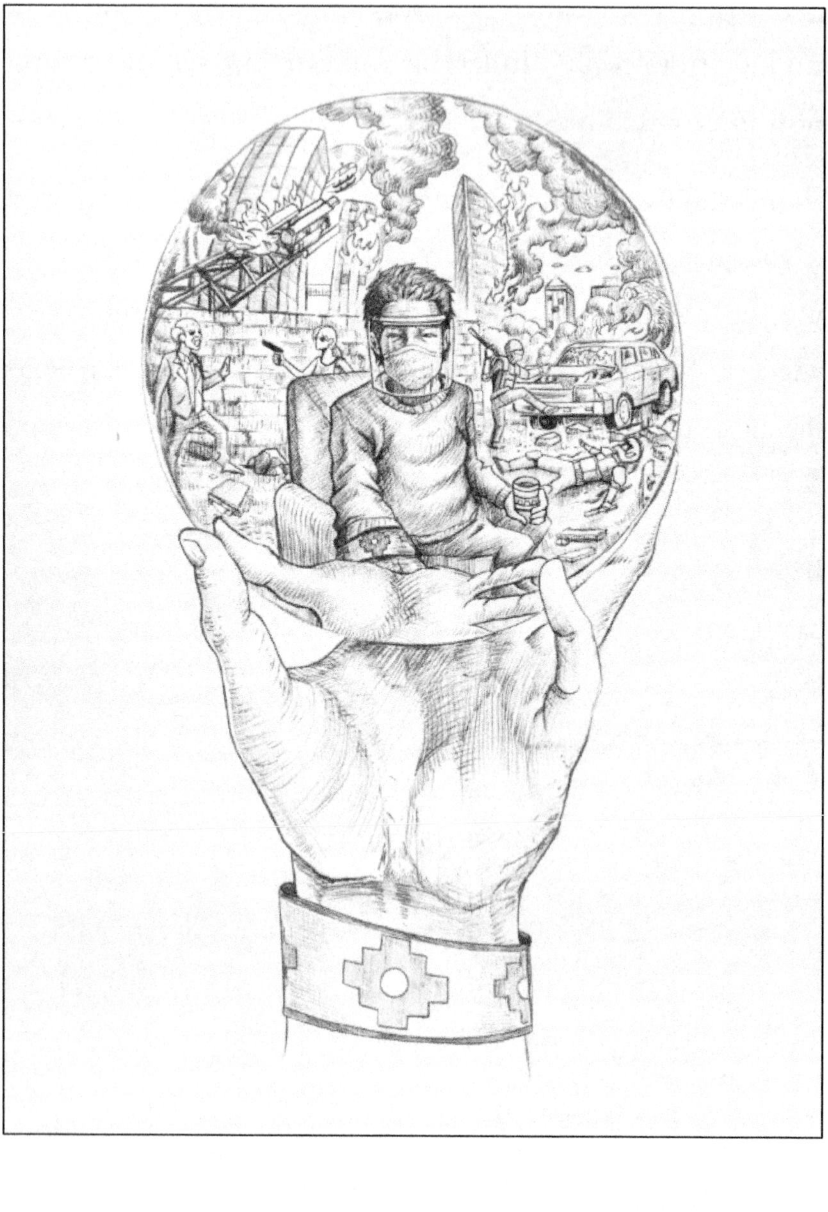

PART I

SHAMANIC HEALING IN MY LIFE AND WORK

CHAPTER 1

2020, THE YEAR OF CHAOS AND GREAT OPPORTUNITY

Since my early childhood, I was fascinated with stories of people who could see the future. From Biblical prophets to Nostradamus and Baba Vanga, we read about people who had a certain ability to predict future events. I was interested in the paranormal from a very early age. I was especially obsessed with clairvoyance. One thing I remember clearly contemplating is that if clairvoyance is real and the future can be predicted, does it not mean that the future is predetermined? How otherwise can one predict something that has many variables? And if the future were already decided, can I change it? These questions, among others, tormented my mind.

Growing up in the Soviet Union, a spiritual desert under the Iron Curtain of a socialist regime, was the last place that any answer to such things would be found. An atheist society in which religious sentiment of any kind was a social crime was not a fertile ground where my imagination could sprout. There was nothing in my world to even spark these kinds of ideas. Their source is still unclear.

My interest in the paranormal was fueled by reading science fiction books. As a child, I found joy in entertaining myself imagining having the ability to fly, to move through walls, to be invisible, to communicate with others in my dreams and to read people's minds. I remember sitting in a classroom in third grade, thinking that if I could read the teacher's mind, I could easily pass the exam. I never was a good student. I was bored in school. To me it was mental torture. I was growing up with the hope that one day I would find something that would make my life meaningful. I heard a calling but didn't know where it was coming from.

The Cactus of Sanity

I was about 10 years old when I was training with the football team. One day, our instructor brought a stencil with the word "Puma" and an image of a jumping puma that we were supposed to spray black paint over on our t-shirts. I still recall the smell of this paint and the feeling I had seeing the Puma on my t-shirt after removing the stencil. This event would be too insignificant to remember, but 23 years later I moved to a small town in the Peruvian Andes, 7,433 miles away, that has a big statue of a puma at its entrance. I didn't even make this connection until years later.

In the Andean cosmology of three worlds, the puma represents the middle world, the world of the Earth. The lower world is represented by a serpent and the higher world is represented by a condor. The middle world, represented by Puma, signifies our life on Earth and our relationship with the world. Could it be that my future was already reaching me in my past by sending me a puma note?

Today, looking back into my past, I feel like growing up was a process of returning to myself, coming home after a long journey. It is my feeling that this new relation with myself and the world was conceived during the three hellish days I spent near death fighting for my life during a Peyote ceremony in Mexico in 2008. At its peak I was stung by a few deadly scorpions. This experience fundamentally changed something in me. I didn't acquire any psychic capabilities as a result of this peril, nor was I endowed with superhuman strength, the ability to climb walls, jump off roofs or fire sticky webs out of my hands like Spider-Man. The transformation occurred in a more subtle, yet profound, way.

I simply understood what's real in life and what actually matters. Above all, it cured the fear of death I had had since very early childhood. Following this dramatic experience, my obsession with the afterlife that had preoccupied me until that point disappeared. Staring at the abyss while dying, I realized that all I wanted and sought was to be found right here, in life, not after. Living fully and consciously before dying became a task of utmost importance. My grip on reality became less fantastic yet more sobering. It may be fair to say that I began to live after nearly dying. (I share this story in great detail in my first book, *PATH: Seeking Truth in a World of Lies*, if you would like to know more about it.)

The obsession with acquiring psychic abilities was now replaced with self-awareness and a strong sense of connection to myself and the world I live in. I felt like I had settled in a certain place, somewhere deep inside my consciousness, where being peaceful, present and aware was enough. From this place I had a stronger connection and a better view of myself and my relation to the world. This serene and grounded existence has become the source of daily joy. An ongoing shamanic practice serving Huachuma cactus, also known as San Pedro, has cemented my place in this world. Today I understand that this feeling of being connected to Spirit is by far more important than an acquisition of any psychic abilities. What is the point of being able to move objects with your mind but remaining static in your understanding?

This being said, prophetic visions of a future received from Huachuma cactus are important, even though they can be very disturbing. I describe the first one I received, a vision in which a dystopian technological future took over humanity, in my second book, *The Mescaline Confession: Breaking through the World of Delusion*. I end *The Mescaline Confession* by speaking of the cosmic virus, suggesting using Nature and plant medicine as an antidote to it. Ironically, this current book also originates from a virus, the coronavirus. If before this was merely a suggestion, today it is a necessity, if you would like to keep your sanity. The umbilical cord with Nature that materialist culture, science and religion has severed must be reestablished. If, in *The Mescaline Confession*, I only advised people to retreat to Nature, then in this book I urge you to do it. More chaos is ahead.

I always end a year and start the next with a ceremony. The ceremony on December 31 is important to say goodbye to the passing year and express gratitude for what it has brought. The next day, on January 1, I do a ceremony to welcome the new year and express my intention for it. I've been doing it for over a decade now. This time, the ceremony

The Cactus of Sanity

on January 1, 2020 was different. During it, I felt like the air of the world was literally filled with lead or iron, it felt so heavy. War-like energies were entering the space. I saw our world as though it were the Titanic approaching an iceberg. I saw the raging havoc coming that would change the way we live. This was a very difficult and disturbing vision that I could not shake out of my head. The same day, after the ceremony, I briefly shared this vision on my Facebook page. A few days later, still feeling the same heaviness and urgency to share it widely, I decided to write an article and choose January 12 for a publication date in order to align my message with the planetary conjunction that brought Saturn and Pluto together.

When I wrote my article, "2020 The Year of Chaos and Great Opportunities,"[3] I wasn't sure where to put the word "great" in the title. I felt strongly that it should go before the word "chaos" but I didn't want to come across as an alarmist. It took me a couple of days to decide. I chose a lighter version of it and placed it before the word opportunity, with an intent to sound more hopeful. Here I would like to reproduce the article entirely as it was published on January 12, 2020.

"In the way that you might look at a glass of water and think it either half-empty or half-full, the year 2020 can be viewed similarly. I see it as a great opportunity for healing and change. Let me explain.

In 1915, right before the devastating, fateful Russian revolution of 1917, the Caucasian mystic George Ivánovich Gurdjieff was engaged in a conversation with Peter D. Ouspensky. Gurdjieff developed what is known as the "Fourth Way" system, which Ouspensky popularized in the West. Ouspensky recorded this conversation in his book *In Search of the Miraculous*.

In it, Gurdjieff claims that esoteric knowledge is material and, like any matter, is limited in quantity and quality at a given space and time. For example, he refers to the number of sand particles on the beach and amount of water in the ocean. Although these seem to be great in number, still this number is limited. The same, he says, is the case with knowledge, and its quality depends on how much is taken from it. He uses gilding as an analogy to support his theory:

"If a certain amount of gold is taken in order to gild other objects and make them look like gold, the more objects there are to be gilded, the less gold will be given to each. If we try to gild more objects, the objects will be covered unevenly and

The Cactus of Sanity

will look worse than objects that weren't touched at all." (Here and below, quoted from P. D. Ouspensky, *In Search of the Miraculous*, 1949)

We can observe this truth among the people who follow different gurus and teachings and think of themselves as very spiritual, different and even superior to the rest of humanity — but, in fact, they appear to be less connected, authentic and sensitive than a person who has never heard about spirituality. But I digress.

Gurdjieff continues: "And on the contrary, the fewer objects that need to be gilded, the more gold they will get. Thus, if a certain amount of knowledge is to be shared among millions of people, this will not be enough to change anything in their lives. As a result, we will lose the gold we originally had. The sharing of knowledge is based on the same principle. If it is given to all, no one gets anything. If it stays among a few, it will be enough not just for personal use but for increasing its supply. If a large amount of knowledge is concentrated in a small number of people, then it will bring great results. From this perspective it is more beneficial to keep the knowledge in a small circle and not spread it into the masses."

This position can explain why esoteric knowledge was hidden in ancient times, available only to initiates. The Eleusinian

Mysteries of ancient Greece and Chavin Mysteries of ancient Peru come to mind. Another intention for hiding this knowledge could be to preserve and protect ancient traditions and rites. This reason relates more to the Christian era, when Christianity began eradicating competing spiritual practices both in Europe and in the Americas during the conquest. But the latter cause does not invalidate the former, and people could be trying to maintain the wholeness of their knowledge and prevent it from misinterpretation and diffusion. Apparently, wise people in ancient times understood this principle: If knowledge is shared among a few, great results can be expected.

Then Gurdjieff speaks about the moral side of this theory. At first glance it appears unfair to those who get nothing. But, in fact, most people do not want any knowledge and thus renounce their own share.

This, he says, "is especially obvious during times of mass psychoses caused by climate change, wars and revolutions, when people lose every bit of sanity and common sense they had in the first place and even the instinct for self-preservation, while turning into robots annihilating one another. As a result, a huge amount of knowledge remains unclaimed and can be shared among those who understand its value. There is nothing unfair about it since those who receive it do not take it from others. No one is taking something that belongs to someone else. Simply put, those who want it find it in abundance, since others have abandoned their shares. They only take that which was left by others and deemed useless, which will be lost anyway if not picked up by someone."

Gurdjieff speaks about the periods in human history when the masses began to destroy centuries or millennia of cultural developments. He says these periods usually match the beginning of the collapse of cultures and civilizations, geological cataclysms and climatic change, during which a tremendous amount of knowledge is being released. This knowledge must be gathered and used or it will be wasted.

I like to think of it as a pouring rain that falls on everyone in town. Only those who gather the rainwater can use it later, perhaps to water their gardens. In a similar way, if we open up to this higher knowledge, we can use it for our personal needs.

"The masses do not want it and do not strive to acquire it, and their leaders, motivated by self-interest, do all they can to increase the fear of the unknown."

Only a small percentage of humanity wants this knowledge. Those who want it, take it, and by doing so they acquire the possibility of becoming more conscious. Not all people can become more conscious, even if they wanted to, Gurdjieff says, because there is an equilibrium that cannot be disrupted. During crises, while the masses are preoccupied with daily survival, the rest find themselves, psychologically, situated among the abandoned treasure, which just needs to be picked up.

Although Gurdjieff's conversation took place over a century ago, today we find ourselves in the exact same situation. Nothing ever changes. Here we are, living in a very unstable world, which reminds me of a ticking time bomb. The eruption of global chaos and the high probability of a civil war in the United States will affect all of us, regardless of where we live. The current climate in the United States and around the world is fermenting towards a violent conclusion. All ingredients are in the pot: fear, hate, anger, anxiety; mental, environmental, economic and political crises; rampant government and corporate corruption; mass protests; the acceleration of the magnetic North Pole shift from the Canadian Arctic towards Russia's Siberia and the three rare planetary conjunctions expected in 2020.

The Cactus of Sanity

Interestingly enough, according to Gurdjieff, all conflicts on Earth are triggered by planets that come too close to each other during their revolutions, sending waves to Earth that manifest in social unrest, wars and revolution. All this is brewing into a perfect storm — but, just as much, into a perfect opportunity as well, if seen in a different way.

It seems like lots of cosmic energy is scheduled to be released. We either harvest it for good or let it be wasted in destruction. Gurdjieff didn't say how this higher knowledge can be reached. He only spoke of its existence and the human condition which he equated to a waking sleep, a hypnotic sleep that continues after we wake up in the morning and go through our day. Gurdjieff called the process of awakening "the work."

It took me a long time to figure this out for myself, something I relate in *The Mescaline Confession*, which takes a deeper look at the sicknesses at the heart of Western culture. The point being, no philosophical system is capable of giving you all you are looking for. At best, it can only point the way and perhaps prepare you for receiving. But receiving what? What is it that everyone is talking about, using different words? Kundalini awakening, enlightenment, Samadhi, etc.: All these different terms describe a state of consciousness and a higher level of being that, they say, is attainable by hard work and life-long spiritual practice — a debatable notion, but that's a subject for another book.

For now, I would only like to say that a path of direct experience is the one I found to be most effective for myself. I found all I ever looked for and even more by walking the shamanic path and working with the plant teachers of the New World: Peyote, Huachuma and Ayahuasca. These are tools that Gurdjieff didn't know about. He never traveled in South America. He traveled in the East, which is well-reflected in his system of thought. He came to North America, but found nothing there except dollars. If he had ever discovered plant medicine, he would never make his students work so hard on themselves to discover nothing at the end, unless he wanted to exploit them. He would send them to Peru to work with plant teachers to find what they were looking for and more.

Perhaps the world was not ready for it then. Perhaps it is not ready for it now. But the time we live in is critical, which creates exceptions to the rule. There is simply no more time for talking about change. There is only time to change. By healing and changing ourselves, the way we live, think and act, we help heal and change the world. We simply need

The Cactus of Sanity

more conscious people in the world to balance the growing insanity.

Here I will stop the references to Gurdjieff and the Fourth Way, for one reason. Although it can be an eye-opener for many, which it certainly was for me 25 years ago, it has its limitations. Perhaps, a century ago, people were not ready for magic, and thus, Gurdjieff's work only existed on a psychological level. It explains the initial magic a person feels when they encounter the Fourth Way. However, as one begins to experience "the work," this feeling vanishes. The "work" is boring. It's like losing a loved one. Life becomes dull and grey.

Nevertheless, the magic exists and can be known. It is alchemy — the true alchemy, understood since the time of Hermes Trismigistus as the esoteric knowledge of transformation, the alchemical change of "lead," the fallen state of humankind, or "the waking sleep", into "gold," humans' spiritual consciousness before the Fall. (The naïve notion of transforming physical lead into gold was a PR narrative for general consumption.) Alchemists used matter to produce higher consciousness and escape the mechanical fate of cosmic laws by repairing the broken link between ancient humanity of the Golden Age and their time, an epoch of Renaissance, the Age of Discovery. They believed that the reversal of humankind's fallen state could be accelerated and assisted by the people who became illuminated through hermeticism, science and magic. For this, these magicians were called heretics and hunted by the Catholic Church.

The idea of transformation and illumination was at the center of Gurdjieff's teaching, but without a direct spiritual experience, it remained in a field of words and concepts. And this, in my opinion, is the missing link in the Fourth Way system. Plant medicine is that "outside help" that Gurdjieff said we all need but didn't name the source. I'm not pointing fingers here, just taking a step further. The era of words and concepts is over. In fact, this over-conceptualization of reality led us to the mess we are in. It's time for direct spiritual experience, which alone has the power to break through dogmas and lead us to an understanding.

To make this subject easier, I suggest replacing the term "esoteric knowledge" with "healing energy," a certain type of energy that we need in order to heal ourselves and deepen our understanding. In our time, this concept is more relatable. This type of energy is highly intelligent, and it knows what you need. You can get in touch with it if you come to it in a sincere and respectful way. Plant medicine shamanism provides all a person needs to instantly see themselves as they are and to make changes in their lives according to their own new vision. Its self-empowering method has been used for thousands of years all across the planet. This regenerating process is simply needed to survive the mass psychoses that are now engulfing the world, to retain sanity and mental health, and to come through it as a better, stronger and more connected human being. You need your body, mind and spirit to be strong and healthy to survive the turbulent times ahead.

Unfortunately, there is simply not enough Huachuma cacti growing in the Andes, Ayahuasca vine in the Amazon or Peyote growing in Mexico to help everyone on Earth. It is simply impossible. In fact, as the demand grows and more people find healing and awakening using plant medicine, the supply is depleting, and it will be harder and more expensive to do this work in the future. My friends, Ayahuasca shamans, are telling me already that they need to go further into the rainforest to find the plants. Plant medicine is for a small percentage of people who are ready to receive it at this time, maybe tens of thousands but certainly not millions. Call them lucky, fortunate or chosen, but the fact of the matter is that plant teachers can only help a certain number of people during a certain period of time. It is in this sense that the knowledge, or the healing energy, is limited, not that it is limited in its capacity to heal and teach. This, I believe, is infinite.

This is your true opportunity to learn about yourself and the world you live in. While it's available, make use of it. Taking advantage of a window of great opportunity to heal and grow spiritually through natural means is a moral choice each of us can make. But any opportunity has its time, and this no exception. As the pandemic and quarantine have proven, your life could change at any time in a way that perhaps makes traveling to Peru no longer possible, and all you will be left with are the books written by people whose lives were actually transformed by these ancient mysteries. Reading them is still a better use of your time than scrolling through Facebook posts, but embracing the knowledge yourself and experiencing it first-hand is far more beneficial.

Today, we are forced into a closer, more intimate relationship with our digital companions, phones and computers. Being locked in our home, we find a sort of a relief in communication that has been severed by the quarantine, social distancing and isolation rules. Perhaps now

The Cactus of Sanity

we understand the simple joy of taking a walk outside, talking to one another in person, shaking hands, hugging and breathing the air without a mask.

Why do we only learn to appreciate things when we lose them? It's a tragedy that has to be reversed. What can be learned from the current situation depends on the individual, but it can be put into practice for self-growth. The crisis will be over, and we will be allowed outside to live our lives again. Will we live differently, with more awareness and gratitude? This question is yet to be answered by each of us when the opportunity presents itself.

2020 is the time for spiritual harvest, healing and growth. Visit us in Peru to work with the sacred plant-teacher Huachuma, also known as San Pedro, which can help you see your inner self just as you see yourself in a mirror. You can shed your old skin like a serpent, leaving confusion and pain in the past. It is an opportunity to reclaim your mind from political and religious paradigms, reconnect with nature, and absorb the strong energies of Huachuma medicine and cosmic influences for healing and personal change. As our world sinks into madness, mental and spiritual health become the highest priority."

A real change becomes possible when we make a commitment to change. It's a personal process of inner growth that happens in spite of the obstacles and difficulties that life presents us on our paths. We can use the current crisis to become better and stronger human beings, or fall backwards. The choice is ours and the time is now.

CHAPTER 2

THE SHAMANIC BRIDGE TO A BETTER FUTURE

Discovering a country with such a rich history as Peru can be a heart- and mind-opening experience. The Amazon rainforest offers its mysteries to those who want to feel like Indiana Jones; while the coast of Peru and the Andes are waiting for people interested in ancient cultures that have preceded one another since the dawn of human civilization. Even if you travel without a specific reason or intention, it will still be an enriching journey into an enchanting world with a vast, colorful and fascinating history.

Traveling is like having a mild psychedelic experience available at any time, no matter where you live. It enables us to see the world in a different way and, hence, the way that we see ourselves. You can always embark on a journey to see the world beyond your local limits. Andre Gide, French author and winner of the Nobel Prize in Literature in 1947, said, "Man cannot discover new oceans unless he has the courage to lose sight of the shore." That is so true, both for earthly discoveries and those made with your mind.

However, instead of just booking a trip to go sit on a beach, which is nice and sometimes needed, what if you could add a deeper purpose to your travel and form a sincere desire to understand yourself and your place in the Universe? What if you could find answers to your big questions and gain clarity about where your life is heading?

This is one aspect of shamanic healing that we focus on at Huachuma Wasi, but the spectrum of healing is wide. We all understand that healing, in a physical sense, means the removal of pain in the body. When you have broken a bone, with time the bone mends, and when you can start using it again, you know it has healed. However, the healing of an emotional wound is different. The pain of losing a loved one can take years to heal. Time is a great healer, that is true, but even time takes time to heal. We can be affected mentally and suffer from anxiety, depression, fear and suicidal thoughts. Healing, in this case, is when you can look at your pain without feeling it. The scar in your heart will remain, but it is no longer bleeding. Healing has taken place when, instead of feeling hopeless, worthless, pessimistic, guilty, and chronically fatigued, one is hopeful, self-confident, optimistic and full of energy to live one's life.

But what is spiritual healing? What or who is actually sick?

The Cactus of Sanity

During my years running a retreat center, all kinds of people have visited. Among them were very rich people who have achieved all their life's material goals. Yet still, they came depressed and even suicidal. Why? Because they realized that, after buying properties all over the world, they still could not buy a bridge towards themselves. Thus, though their bodies were well-fed, their souls were hungry. What do all your possessions matter without meaning and purpose in your life? Your life is empty, causing spiritual pain.

Plant teachers can fix this broken link with yourself, reclaim the sense of magic and wonder you had in your childhood, and reestablish a sense of inner unity. This is shamanic healing, which brings total awareness to the inner content of your life. This inner content is like the files on a computer's hard drive. These files become more accessible by increasing self-awareness and enhancing our human experience on a daily basis. The intensity of our existence is what makes our memory stronger, while self-awareness gives us the capacity to experience this intensity.

A body without self-awareness is like the scenery observed by people who suffer from Alzheimer's disease, a terrible condition affecting the memory. Imagine self-awareness as the operating system of a computer, which makes it possible to organize and access the files stored on its hard drive — its inner content. When someone suffers from Alzheimer's, it is as though there is a disconnect or severe malfunction within the operating system. It is unable to read the files stored in the memory — or perhaps the files themselves have been corrupted and are no longer readable. This condition is not yet fully understood by modern science.

To a much lesser degree we can observe this situation in our culture, where people are hardly aware of themselves. They know where they parked their car, where they left their keys, but not where their heart or happiness are. They know their names and addresses but have forgotten themselves, living their lives as robots in an increasingly mechanical world, functioning without self-awareness. This disconnection from self creates stress, confusion, anxiety, fear and depression, which Western medicine doesn't have a cure for beyond psychological cosmetic makeup. Pharmaceutical drugs are only capable of masking the symptoms while leaving the root cause unaddressed and presenting a number of negative side effects as our sensitive biology struggles to process these unnatural chemicals.

Modern psychiatry does not believe in the soul. How can you cure something that you don't believe exists? The soul is a

The Cactus of Sanity

vague concept, and arguing about it leads either nowhere or towards violence. It is the same thing as asking if there is a God. Bypassing theological debate about the existence of the soul, let's just call it "consciousness" — that is, having a human experience. The point being, we often spend a lot of time and energy asking questions that simply cannot be answered. Would it not be a better use of your time to focus on what actually matters in your life? For example, what prevents you from being happy? Modern medicine does not have a cure for Alzheimer's disease, and psychiatry does not have a cure for depression, but the majority of humanity can be helped.

There is a general misconception and confusion about plant medicines being dangerous and harmful, but this fear is rooted in a lack of understanding and expertise. Somehow, Huachuma has the power to bring to the surface and make understandable what has long been forgotten or deemed insignificant. This understanding heals the spirit, which Western medicine denies the existence of. Through many years of working with the Huachuma cactus, I have observed tremendous psychological healing as well as improved physical health, for me and many who have come to Huachuma Wasi. Half-jokingly, I call the cactus the "memory restoration agent."

The clarity of thought and beauty that Huachuma medicine cultivates is the healing. In practical terms, this clarity allows you to examine your life very closely and see what is not helping you — that is, what is blocking you from being happy, whether this is internal or external, such as patterns of behavior and personal habits, or your job, relationships, etc. The medicine gives you a new perspective. This ultimately allows you to make better decisions that improve the quality of your life and wellbeing.

You can verify this for yourself at Huachuma Wasi, a treasure island for creative minds and an oasis for the seeker. Over ten years, my wife and I have transformed a corn field into a beautiful space for guests to enjoy and explore, relax, think creatively, and heal themselves. Many of those who come to visit extend their stay longer than planned, sometimes considerably so. You can come and stay with us at any time. The only commitment you have to make is to yourself and your own healing, while we provide support and assistance in whatever way we can. Our ceremonies take place every two days all year around.

One of our guests was a man who apparently was a bit concerned prior to taking the medicine with us. He told me that he read trip reports online and was very curious about the experience but was afraid he might lose his mind. I assured him that his safety and sanity were guaranteed. He trusted me and came for a ceremony. During the course of the day, at the river where we often do ceremonies, we talked. At one point in our conversation, he said that the Huachuma experience was the sanest experience in his life. We both laughed. It was so indeed. Huachuma is an antidote to confusion. I only added later that I see Huachuma as an insurance policy for our sanity, an insurance agent you are always happy to see.

A couple of years ago, a therapist from California in his late 50s or early 60s, whose expertise was in family, marriage and adolescent therapy, visited our center. We spoke about many things during his stay with us, among them, psychiatry. When he told me that the pharmaceutical industry had taken the therapy out of therapy, it was easy for me to agree. I cannot say that this was news to me. From my own understanding, I had come to a similar conclusion. Unfortunately, this is the reality of the modern world.

During our last ceremony, he said something that truly touched me. We sat by the river, a beautiful place where we find the most peace and healing energies. We were talking about plant medicine shamanism and its potential for healing, which psychiatry generally overlooks or rejects. I explore this in depth in *The Mescaline Confession*. Here I will only share this story to make a point. He said to me that one ceremony with me was worth five years of therapy. These were strong words. A therapist with a decade of study and years of practice admitted to the healing potential of Huachuma in such a direct way. Five years of therapy in a day! Just think about it. Could it be that Western medicine's overall negative attitude towards plant-based shamanism is based in fear of competition? How can they compete if what takes five years is accomplished in a day?

After a long pause spent in silence, he added that as a psychotherapist, he just can't advise his clients to leave their desk, go out to Nature and dance. I shared with him that at some point in my life I was considering taking the professional path of mainstream psychology, following my passion for healing through human connection. He replied that he was glad that I didn't pursue it as a career and added, "You are doing more now." Interestingly enough, a few years later I had a similar conversation with another person at the same place, who during a ceremony told me the same thing, only from the perspective of a patient. He said that one Huachuma ceremony could counted for five years of therapy.

The Cactus of Sanity

He spoke from experience. He had struggled with depression for many years and had a therapist. This was a powerful confirmation.

I felt like sharing with him further that what brought me to shamanism was not a search for healing. I was physically and mentally healthy. I was led by a burning desire to find truth and meaning in my life. I wanted to find answers to big questions, answers that no one else could give it to me. Good mental health is a baseline, a necessary condition to be fulfilled in order for a person to reach higher consciousness. Often it comes together. Healing and insights are friends. But sometimes it takes time to find psychological ground to stand on before entering a realm of mysticism and magic.

I said that I focus my work on a spiritual connection that, I believe, leads to healing. A suffering soul makes the body ill. Psychiatry, I said, seems to ignore the very notion of the soul and treats the person like a machine. This approach, I felt, was insufficient. He agreed. Another therapist, with a doctorate in psychology, came to stay for three months. He said his time at Huachuma Wasi, besides being insightful and revealing, also saved his life.

It is difficult to convey the feeling when, after a Huachuma ceremony, before going to bed, I check the news to see what is happening in the world. I like to be updated on world events. I don't even need to read news anymore. I know what's in it by simply reading the headlines. The contrast between a day of beauty, peace and magic spent outdoors and the headline is striking. Sometimes I do it just for fun. Sometimes reading news after the ceremony is simply hilarious. It feels like I am observing life on some distant planet when mental patients have escaped the asylum, changed clothes and made the rest of the people believe that they are their leaders. The absurdity gets so great that often I wake up my wife at night trying to suppress my giggles.

After searching the web for some time, I retreat back to myself with ever greater gratitude to have Huachuma medicine in my life. I walk outside and sit in our garden. Fascinated by the night sky and mesmerized by the magical crickets' chirp, I stare into the abyss while thinking about the brief moment we call life. There is so much to be done in such a short time. As much as we need a cure for cancer, we need a cure for our stupidity.

Other times, the news is tragic and painful. In *The Mescaline Confession* I spoke about the efforts of psychiatrists of the first half of the 20th century to understand schizophrenia. It seems as though, since then, schizophrenia has escaped the

The Cactus of Sanity

walls of confinement. Today, not only is it easily seen anywhere you look, but worse, it has become more and more culturally accepted.

Many people want to see change in the world, but how many people want to make change within themselves? When you change yourself, you affect others in a positive way. This is the only chain reaction that we want to see taking place on the planet. Whether you are a seeker of truth and are tired of hearing about "awakening" and "enlightenment," or you are a curious traveler who just learned about plant-based shamanism, Huachuma Wasi can help you on your path. There are many different ways of working with plant medicines and no written rule as to how to do so. The ancient ways of working with Huachuma have nearly been lost. We don't know exactly what was happening three thousand years ago at the Temple of Chavin, the cradle of Andean Huachuma shamanism, but from the little knowledge that we do have, deep and strong new roots are grown.

We do not throw you straight into the deep end of the pool with the strongest medicine that we make. Rather, we guide you through the process step by step as we teach you how to "swim" and develop a connection with the medicine in your own unique way. We only give you what you need and can handle. We work with the medicine by spending lots of time out in Nature sitting in silence, which becomes the medium for healing. Silence is a door to understanding. Time spent here is productive.

Huachuma lifts you up and lets you see your life from a distance, allowing for all aspects to be seen from a greater perspective. By transcending your own fears, you embrace your own power. With it comes a sense of responsibility over your life. This is what I call "humanized spirituality." Not a mental practice or a system of belief, but a constant and conscious engagement with life.

CHAPTER 3

ENVISIONING YOUR LIFE

I remember the day my wife and I sat on the ground in what at the time was a corn field and looked at Apu Pitusiray, a massive mountain with seven visible peaks. I was telling her about our family's future house, which would be a retreat center as well, all built here where we sat. At that time we didn't have any money and my words were a mere dream. But my wife believed me. My vision was clear, my will determined. I knew this would be done. And it has been done in the exact way I envisioned it, though the road was rather bumpy.

In 2011 I got a call from a Russian guy who had only one day in the Cusco region. A friend had referred him, and he wanted to do a ceremony with me. I agreed, and we went to a nearby sacred site to spend the day with the medicine. During our conversation on the way, he said that he owned a publishing house in Moscow. I told him that I was thinking of writing a book but didn't have anyone to present it to, and if he would take a look, I would sit down and write. He agreed. We spent a beautiful day in the mountains. He said he would be back.

After he left, I began writing my first book, *PATH: Seeking Truth in a World of Lies*. When I finished, I sent him the file. He read it and liked it. He said it's definitely a book, and we are going to publish it. I was so excited. He asked me if I would be willing to come to Moscow for a book presentation. I said, of course, if my travel expenses would be taken care of. At that time, I couldn't afford a meal in a restaurant. My wife was breastfeeding and couldn't work. Our first daughter was one year old. I was the only breadwinner in the family. During this time, visitors to

The Cactus of Sanity

Huachuma Wasi were rather sporadic, and it was barely enough to make a living.

Three months passed and finally I received an edited copy of my book. I could not read more than 30 pages. I couldn't recognize my own story. It was distorted with lies that never happened. How could a book with the subtitle, "Seeking Truth in a World of Lies," be full of lies? I literally felt hurt in my heart. I wrote back and said that this is not my book, and I can't let it be published the way it is. It had to be the way I wrote it. The publisher explained that they were preparing a commercial product suitable for the public, and I could get my first payment in a month if I agreed to publication. I had to refuse the offer, even though I only had 30 dollars in my pocket, all our savings at the moment.

I told my wife. She was upset by the news. She was more practical and had our baby, who needed diapers, in her hands. I explained to her that I wouldn't care if I were selling a novel, but this was the true story of my life, which I wanted to share with other spiritual seekers who, just like me, were searching for truth and meaning. It was important for me to keep it honest. She understood and supported me. Originally, I wrote it in Russian, but after I broke with him, I translated it into English myself, making sure the translation was correct. I didn't want anyone to twist my thoughts again.

Years passed and my vision was manifesting itself. The first house was built on the land. It took us 10 years to complete our project. The vision I had became a reality. What is magic if not a vision plus action? What is magic if not clarity plus will? Huachuma allows you to find your life vision and enhances your ability to move towards it. It is up to you to achieve it. The medicine does not impose anything but only reveals the path of clarity, while leaving us the choice to act or not.

You will never know if there is a book in you unless you start writing. *Write Your Zen in 30 Days*[4] is a small workbook for spiritual seekers to complete. I wrote it in three hours during a ceremony, from envisioning the cover to the last word. I recorded all the quotes exactly as they came to me during the ceremony. It is a self-filling container, the contents of which can help people better understand themselves. I encourage people to commit to a small task on a paper and maintain their will throughout the process. Just a page a day might help enhance one's concentration and form a new, good habit.

The Cactus of Sanity

Envision and move courageously toward your goals in life. Nothing is a greater obstacle than your own fear and self-doubts. They discourage you from pursuing your dreams and living a happy, healthy life. They ruin your relationship and friendships. They hurt your productivity. Fear is a thief of your dreams and a killer of your peace. The battle is in your head. End it right there. Feel love instead.

School doesn't teach us how to live fulfilling lives. We are taught that money equals success, when in fact success is when you live your life the way you want, regardless of how much money you have in the bank. I've met a number of people over the years who had lots of money, multimillionaires even, but were unhappy, misguided and depressed. Money alone didn't buy them happiness.

Changing your life takes as much will-power as a rocket breaking through the gravitational field of the Earth and launching into space. A rocket encounters the most resistance when it's near the Earth's surface. The planet's force of gravity pulls the rocket downward even as the air makes it harder to climb. But as the rocket moves higher, the force of gravity diminishes, and as the air gets thinner, the resistance pushing against the rocket gets lower. The most amount of fuel is needed at the start, to launch the rocket. Huachuma is the booster that can help launch yourself into a better, healthier and happier life, into your spiritual orbit. It's the fuel you need to break through self-destructive habits that hold you back, like gravity pulls the rocket towards the ground.

By this, I don't mean only physiological addictions that are more visible, like drugs and alcohol, but also the psychological addictions to fear, worry, self-doubt. This self-diminishing thinking is a major block on the road to happiness and success in life. It dulls the vision and weakens the will. Huachuma medicine can fix it for you, but it's up to you to maintain the new lifestyle. Your participation is required in the process of healing and growth. The medicine is the launching pad, but when you are in the air, the navigation comes back to you. The decisions you make from that point are your responsibility. The medicine should not be blamed in case you fail to maintain your new vision and way of life. Huachuma pauses your life to let you see how it is going.

Without a life vision, you are like a dry leaf lifted by the wind and dropped when the wind retreats. Challenges are opportunities for growth, if you are willing to overcome them. Experience and understanding are your reward. By

The Cactus of Sanity

hiding from challenges, you are narrowing the possibilities in your life. Vision is not everything, but it's what you need in order to achieve what you want. Courage, love and trust in yourself are the great allies on your path.

CHAPTER 4

THE SOURCE OF INNER PEACE

"Nothing can bring you peace but yourself. Nothing can bring you peace but the triumph of principles."

— Ralph Waldo Emerson

As a lifelong spiritual seeker of truth and meaning in life, I can say with certainty that finding inner peace is the goal of spiritual search. It's a place where you reunite with your soul. You become who you always were but with a deep feeling of contentment. Your familiar self that has wondered and pondered, traveled and suffered, is finally mature. This is not to say that the learning has ended. I feel like the learning process is ongoing and will continue for as long as I live. Learning is a habit that I've formed throughout my life, truly a good one compared to all the destructive habits I had to let go of. However, from this point I see it more as curiosity about the world than a necessity for my soul. I will develop this subject in my next book, which I want to dedicate to all spiritual seekers who find themselves stuck in cults, burdened by ideologies and suffering from a guru syndrome. Here I

The Cactus of Sanity

only want to speak about it in the context of what it means to be human, as opposed to becoming a machine.

I am at peace with myself. I am content being myself. I can live without any new input. In a spiritual sense, I have become self-sustainable, like a cactus. It is an amazing feeling. Being a human means feeling the whole range of emotions. Of course, feeling positive emotions is more pleasant and nourishing, but even the negative emotions make us who we are and can be used to fuel change.

I'll give you an example. Growing up in the Soviet Union in a working class family, I didn't know hunger, but we lived within our means and had the necessities. Later, when we immigrated to Israel, we embraced the fate of immigrants. When I moved to the United States and became a slave in a Fellowship of Friends cult, poverty finally became my enemy. Hardship may have a certain value during the time of character formation, but it becomes a burden on a man's soul when he is mature enough to walk the path of life with purpose.

I had to use the power of my anger to change things. I felt that poverty was humiliating my spirit and limiting the expression of my creativity. Instead of giving into self-pity, thinking, "Why was I born in the Soviet Union and in a family of working people, instead of being born in a middle or upper class family and in a free country, with much more of a head start from the beginning?" I felt grateful for being born where I was and into the family I had. My place of birth drove me and my family gave me a solid education in love. My parents loved one another, and both my sister and I were born in that nest. We had love from the start. Love is what I remember. This warm feeling is what kept my relationship with my parents throughout my life, regardless how far I physically went from my parental home. This love is what teaches me how to be a parent today, giving love to my children, perhaps even more since I am more expressive by nature. Although I had loving parents, they were not self-expressive. I don't know if this was a cultural phenomenon, or it was only true to my folks. But the fact remains they were not expressive in words. I grew up like them, not being able to express my love to them. I never told my father that I loved him, and I only said it once to my mother, on her deathbed, fighting an aggressive cancer, when she already was unconscious. It is painful to admit it and to live with it. Some things cannot be changed.

I've made peace with my past and turned my demons into friends. The past I was ashamed of and tried to escape is now

The Cactus of Sanity

serving me well, helping me help others who feel lost in their lives. I've been in many people's shoes, and I know how it feels not knowing your path and being indifferent to your life. I know how it feels when you see people getting ahead while leaving you behind. I know how it feels to be lonely and misunderstood. I know how it feels to fall into drugs and be hopeless. I've been there. I've done it. But I stood up and just said no. There is a future that I yearn for. And so my intentional journey began.

Over the years I've helped many people find their path in life: to stop being self-destructive, to quit drugs and alcohol abuse, to find purpose and creativity, to repair family connections and personal relations. I encouraged many to embrace life and live from a place of love, not fear. A number of guests came with their family members, which was so beautiful to watch.

But I failed in something that is impossible to fix: to bring this medicine to my parents. I could have helped them live and die in peace. But the physical distance was too great, and I didn't have the resources to make this happen. They lived in Israel, I in Peru. The Pacific Ocean kept us apart from one another. They both died horrible deaths, tortured by cancer and chemotherapy. If nothing else, the medicine could have helped them so much to prepare for the final journey from life. But this didn't happen.

The second pain is the fact that they didn't live long enough to see me happy, to see me finally settled. We used to meet on Skype weekly. My older daughter was just a few years old. They loved her. But they died before my second daughter was born. Back then, we still were struggling as a young family, trying to build our life from scratch.

This pain is partly eased. At least they knew my wife and my older daughter. But how different it would be to meet now, when the struggle is behind us, and we live in our beautiful place, a nest for our children to grow in love. How happy they would be to see us happy at last and to see me finally maturing and finding myself and my place in life.

I compensate for it by expressing my love constantly to my wife and my children. I feel like my parents' love for me and their trust in me were the main guides on my soul-searching path. These very human feelings were the ground I stood on even when I felt like falling; the same ones I want to give to my children so they feel loved even more. It's encouraging and empowering. Feelings are what makes us human. One can argue that it is just an impulse, an electromagnetic signal that is translated by our brain into feeling of love, but that

The Cactus of Sanity

would be like thinking that the warming sunlight that you pleasantly feel on your body while lying on the beach is just gamma ray radiation that penetrates a cosmic vacuum to reach you with the danger of giving you skin cancer. This scientific approach will ensure your absence from the beach and deprive you of the soul-healing feeling that you feel lying there. And the calming sound of incoming waves would hardly matter if you perceive it as a vibration that reaches your ear and is translated by your brain into sound.

This scientific interpretation steals the magic of life, a self-imposed robbery that scientifically-oriented minds suffer from. They don't actually live. They simply exist in the quantum cosmic soup while trying to figure out the recipe of their existence. To me not only is it boring but tragic. Lacking the sense of magic, no wonder why some of them want to become robots and digits and escape the "boredom" of being human, not realizing that their boredom is rooted in their perception, not biology. Our human biology is incredible. It allows for direct perception of Divine when tuned. It allows for love, joy and spiritual contentment that guard us against a suicidal transhumanist cult led by atheist technocrats. Bittersweet soul searching is what makes us human. Robots have no search. They do what they are programmed to do. They are autonomous droids who are built to function. They are the actors who never realize they're acting. They are not supposed to. But we do. We are the creatures endowed with consciousness, a function of the soul. We are here to love, learn and grow spiritually. We are here to merge with Divine, not a machine. A merger with a machine is a dead end for the soul. It's where the human journey ends. It's where we die. Transhumanism is a self-extermination cult.

Huachuma has reaffirmed everything I ever felt about what it means to be alive and took me further on my quest for self-discovery. To me it is an Earthlink and an anchor for organic life, the opposite direction from transhumanism. Huachuma has helped me love my body, love my spirit. It has reinforced my connection with myself and my relationship with existence. I am happy to be human, and I am happy to be me. Sergey Baranov a cyborg? What a joke!

We are privileged to live in the 21st century, but not because we have technology in our life — this, in fact, might do more harm than good — but because we live in a crucial time where the direction for our species is being now decided. We actually have a duty and obligation to contribute to the thousands of years of collective evolution and soul searching

The Cactus of Sanity

by making a stand. Do we betray the ancient philosophers and thinkers who dedicated their lives trying to understand human nature and give up on humanity, or do we add value to it by embracing it and emphasizing its value? This historical moment is just as important for collective evolution as it is important for personal evolution. It's a defining moment for our spirit. Whether we win or lose the war for humanity depends on how quick we reach a critical mass of awakened people.

CHAPTER 5

I WANT TO BE ME

If we don't know who we are, we can assume any role, no matter how destructive it might be to our true self. "Who am I?" is the most important question one can ask in this life. It was the first question I asked myself when I was a child. This question felt more important than any input I was receiving from the outside world. In fact, I felt the incoming signals were distracting me from pondering this question and simply being myself.

I remember one occasion when I was eight years old, in the Second Grade. I was in an art class, the only class besides sport I truly liked to attend. All the students were asked what they would like to be when they grew up. Those the teacher called had to stand up and reply. Doctor, engineer, football player, truck driver, painter, the kids answered.

I was sitting in the very back of the room, at the last table, a place reserved for bad students. I was called last and asked the same question. When I stood up, I only said that I want to be me. This caused laughter among the students in the classroom. I felt embarrassed. I sat down and looked out the window. The outside world felt more real than the laughter in the classroom. Perhaps this somewhat traumatic memory had fueled my path to self-discovery.

Looking back at my childhood, I now think that I always was living in a different dimension. I was going to school, playing football, and doing all the same things as everyone else, but at the same time I was mesmerized by the sounds of crickets at night, by the change of seasons, by the snowy winter mornings before the sunrise, by the shimmering stars. I sensed magic everywhere I looked in nature. I felt like I was actually living in all of that and only functioned in the day-to-day world, where going to school and learning about Lenin's Communist party, the Bolshevik revolution, and the proletariat ideology, with which we were brainwashed from an early age, felt like an alien dimension to me.

Then we were taught about the rise of Stalin and the Second World War, senseless events in human history that killed millions and had an impact on millions more. They too seemed to me be some kind of a mistake, a human error that shouldn't have happened. Why were people killing each other? I was asking myself as a kid. Was that necessary? Why couldn't people just live their lives and do what they like? As a kid I didn't understand politics, but I could feel things as they were. I could perceive the energies of people and events in history.

The history of Russia as we were taught in school didn't have any magic in it whatsoever. It was cold, dry and boring. Meanwhile the dimension of life I was living in was warm, fresh and amusing. At some point I thought that retaining this connection throughout my life was the most important thing I could do to myself. Growing up and facing cultural pressure, I always kept my sacred space protected, no matter what. This was my inner world, my connection to life. I was open to new acquaintances and was attracted to people who seemed thoughtful. I was looking for like-minded people with whom I could share the experience of life. All this together formed a strong longing for something outward, which led me to books on occultism, then to esotericism.

I began to think that there must have been an unbroken tradition of truth seekers in human history, people who lived their lives with the same thirst for finding truth and meaning. And it just happened that I was one of them living in the modern world. My circumstances were less than favorable, and I could not see my path behind social obstacles. Today, I think, this was a necessary condition for me to overcome, a payment I had to make to find my path in

The Cactus of Sanity

life. Why is it that we can only connect the dots from future to past? Why not otherwise? Why does life only make sense later, afterwards? How much easier it would be if we could have this reassurance in the present when events happen? Would it not be better if we could maintain that sense of calmness and certainty, knowing that what is happening is all right and cannot be different, because if it could be different it probably would be?

This fascination with life and esoteric teaching led me to join the Fourth Way, which was brought to Russia by G.I. Gurdjieff, whose extensive travel in central Asia, Egypt, Iran, India and Tibet allowed him to assemble certain teachings that, according to him, were able to wake people's conscience and consciousness. His main idea was that people are sleepwalkers, living their life in a dream. Only those who want it and are fortunate to meet a teacher in their life will awaken. In my first book, *PATH*, I describe in detail the six years I spent in Fellowship of Friends, a Fourth Way cult located in Northern California. Withstanding constant brainwashing with crazy, twisted teachings based on Fourth Way ideas but perverted to an unimaginable extent was a battle for my sanity. Coming out of it with my sanity intact was perhaps the most important training I have done in my life, other than nearly dying in Mexico.

The following shamanic endeavor that began in Peru in 2005 has transformed my life, led me out of darkness and into the light. Ayahuasca and Huachuma welcomed me in Peru with Don Howard Lawler, an American who lived in Iquitos for many years. His big smile, wisdom and good medicine pushed me over the cliff of my fears and allowed me to spread my own wings and fly. Don Howard passed away in 2019, but the seeds he planted in me have grown into a beautiful Huachuma garden in the Andes that continues the healing work he began in the rainforest.

The Cactus of Sanity

The shamanic dimension that I found in Peru was beyond all expectations, even though my expectations were high. It was a parallel world that existed within the familiar world and yet was invisible to the naked eye. Giant, endless and mysterious, it was open to be experienced. My first two books were attempts to describe it all, and I'm still trying. I feel so indebted to sacred plant teachers, in particular Huachuma, that I feel trying to convey this to others is simply my duty, and this book is just another attempt to do that.

During the years of reading and taking psychedelics, there were many books that I felt were important and useful on my path. However, only a few had the power to inspire. *Siddhartha*, by Herman Hesse, was one such book for me. It confirmed my feeling that following one's own heart is the path to freedom. Jonathan Swift, the 18th century Anglo-Irish writer, said it best: "May you live every day of your life." So simple and so profound. As a writer myself, I came to appreciate other people's efforts because I know what it takes to write a book or even an essay. Much less do I feel like I can judge great philosophers who dedicated their lives to contemplation and writing. Yet, still, I can humbly suggest my personal take on any given subject due to my sincere search for the truth.

Later, when I began to look into German philosophy and came across the work of Martin Heidegger, I realized that I needed direct experience of Being to understand what it actually meant. Years later, I was already working with the plant teachers of Peru and Mexico, which told me more about Being than I could ever grasp from Heidegger's writings. Huachuma medicine in particular has shown me what it means to be: a direct experience of existence.

According to Heidegger, Being is "the 'most universal,' self-evident and indefinable concept." He is correct. It is a phenomenon that exists in every living thing. Every creature, small or big, exists in time and space. But whether or not it is aware of itself is another question. One can spend a lifetime digging through texts of medieval ontologies and still be unaware of oneself. Self-awareness, or lack thereof, makes the whole difference. "The Self cannot be conceived either as substance or as subject but is grounded in existence." He is correct again. The self can be only felt, and this feeling is the bond it has with existence. Time, Heidegger says, consists of a pure sequence of "nows." Yes, one's life continues now, like a train that appears from afar, passing by with a noise and disappearing into the dark tunnel of the unknown. Ecstasy, he says, means standing outside. He didn't say outside of

The Cactus of Sanity

what, but we can assume it is the standing outside of one's ego or mind and time, touching the heart of existence. Of course, there is a great difference between talking about ecstasy and experiencing it. Most likely Heidegger never experienced it, otherwise he would speak about his experience, for this is something that cannot be forgotten or hidden from others. It bursts out like a plant from the seed.

With Huachuma, I began to feel that even though the study of philosophy was amusing and educating, I no longer needed it to be me. It had become a side dish, a pastry after a main course, while the main course was Beingness itself, the substance for my soul. The very same question that kept great minds like Plato, Aristotle and Heidegger up at night has now been answered without words. Thus, diving into the intellectual abyss was replaced with conscious living.

The theories of German philosophers are still brighter than the depressing Buddhists' tenet of self-denial. Except for Zen, Buddhists look at life as something to escape from rather something to embrace. I don't know at what point people who loved wisdom made such a tragic mistake by looking at the temporal with disdain. Perhaps it is rooted in the fear of death, which choses detachment as a safety mechanism against love. Through the years of working with Huachuma cactus, more and more I came to realize how precious our life is. Its temporal nature makes it special. To be aware and conscious of one's temporality leads to a different quality of being, a place from where you cherish every moment and express your gratitude for the gift of life, however long it may last. Sharing this gift with those whom we love makes life worth living. What is temporal is precious, and how we choose to spend this moment in eternity is all that matters.

If we want to live a fulfilling life, it must be authentic. The problem with our world is that the future becomes a priority. But how will our future be authentic if our present is fake? We have progressed from fake boobs to fake news, fake science, fake food and now even fake people. We have lost the taste for authenticity, which now poses an existential threat to the human species. If we assume that moving towards the future moves us towards our evolved Self, then it becomes clear that the artificial intelligence (AI) enthusiasts are misleading us. We are what we are, living, conscious, empathic organisms, not silicon dummies with microchips. We are not cyborgs or digits on the screen, we are consciousness embedded in a flesh and blood that only has to realize itself as such.

The Cactus of Sanity

Similarly, one of my early childhood obsessions was UFOs and alien life. I held in my hands my very first picture of a UFO when I was about eight years old. I don't remember how I got it, but I brought it home one day from school and looked at it every night before going to sleep. It was a classic-looking flying saucer. It was poor quality in black and white. I remember asking myself as a kid if this were real or not, but regardless, I wanted to believe that it was real. I pondered on it a lot, while looking at the night sky from my window. I thought, where did I come from? Was there a star somewhere that was my home before becoming a human? A thought that wasn't shared among my schoolmates.

This obsession with establishing contact with extraterrestrial life was enhanced further by reading science fiction books. This desire for contact didn't go away for many years and was further enhanced during open-air psytrance parties in Israel and then California. I felt like I was sharing something in common with alien-looking ravers. LSD was certainly something pushing my mind in this direction. But this didn't feel friendly or warm. To my taste, LSD was cold and impersonal and didn't resonate with me much. I didn't trust its origin. It felt synthetic and alien. This was before I began researching the subject, and what I felt was purely intuitive.

Sergey Baranov

This preoccupation with alien life disappeared after my near-death experience in Mexico, along with my fear of death and obsession with the afterlife.

Today, I could care less if I see a lizard-looking alien landing in a sardine container on top of a mountain. I feel too grounded to be bothered. I feel like nothing is more important than loving my family, loving my work and sharing the amazing Huachuma medicine with others. Walking my path in a waking dream, with feet on the ground and head in the sky. Life is magnificent and sacred. The dimension of life, love and plant medicine is rich and inexhaustible.

CHAPTER 6

OBJECTIVE REALITY OF THE HEART

"There is no logical way to the discovery of elemental laws. There is only the way of intuition, which is helped by a feeling for the order lying behind the appearance."

— Albert Einstein

Wisdom that warms the heart is a love affair between poetry and intuition. It is something that is always true. When you are in the moment and aware of yourself, the world becomes poetry and your perception becomes wisdom. This is why it is impossible to learn wisdom in a classroom. You can read about it, you can get familiar with other people's experiences, but eventually you have to find your own. Wisdom is the collection of the profound moments and insights that one receives on the path of pondering and contemplation.

My first taste of wisdom came from my father when I was a kid. He told me about the phrase that was engraved in the Seal of Solomon: "This too shall pass." Even as a kid, these words struck me as eternally truthful. I recalled this phrase often during moments of hardship in my life. Meditating on it helped me see through the temporality of the situation I was in. It made it easier to pass through difficult times. Later on in life, I looked for the source of this phrase.

There's a fable about a powerful king who asked his wise men to create an amulet that will make him happy when he is sad. Following his request, the sages gave him a ring with the Persian words, "This too shall pass," etched on it. This had the desired effect — but it also made him sad when he was happy. Regardless of whether this came from King Solomon himself or originated with Persian Sufis, the truth in it remains intact. Today, looking back, I feel that this phrase cemented in me a desire to find the truth, that which never changes and always is. Perhaps this was a strong motive for me to become a follower of the Fourth Way.

According to G.I. Gurdjieff, objective art is any piece of art — painting, literature, music or monument — that is made consciously and can only be understood objectively as the author intended the work to be understood. I was attracted to Gurdjieff partly because he seemed to understand that there is a timeless reality hidden behind our ordinary waking consciousness, a reality that can be experienced. This spoke to me strongly since I had already experienced psychedelics prior to reading Gurdjieff, and I knew this for a fact. I ended

The Cactus of Sanity

up giving the benefit of the doubt to the teaching that promised to access this higher state of consciousness without substances. Over the years, I came to realize that this promise was an illusion that is generally held among spiritual teachers in order to ensure their following. Otherwise, if one realizes their own divine connection, why follow a guru?

After years of trying, I came back to where I started from. Experimenting with substances has led me to the shamanic path and working with plant teachers, which has brought me closer to what objective reality means for me. Why do I think it is important to speak about it here? Because it confirms the mystical realm, which is elusive and unseen to the rational mind but present when the veil — the intellect — is finally lifted, in order for intuition to see directly into the nature of Reality. This realm can be felt by any sensitive person to a certain extent. However, to touch its depth and feel the feelings behind an expression of it, a certain help is needed. To me, the best medium for that is Huachuma medicine.

I remember lying on the ground during one ceremony and looking at the passing clouds. I could hear a light wind flirting with the eucalyptus leaves and a thought passing through my head: The sky is a daily bread for the soul. It truly was; it was feeding the very fabric of my being, so healing and peaceful. Perhaps a year later, reading the work of Ralph Waldo Emerson, I found the following quote: "The sky is a daily bread for the eyes." And since the eyes are the windows to the soul, essentially we have thought the same thing.

The Cactus of Sanity

Prior to that, I thought that these insights were personal. But now I realized that what is personal is the perception but that which is perceived is objective. Reading Emerson's work further, I found greater resonance with him as a person. How similarly he and I viewed things!

"I like the silent church before the service begins, better than any preaching."

Wisdom and truth permeate this statement, which can alone redefine your sense of spirituality. Objective perception, a part of objective art, is certainly a skill worth developing in life. I believe it is a muscle of our spirit that can be trained and shaped. As I write these words, I stop for a moment to look through my window. I see beautiful mountains as they are. I don't think about them, I don't measure or name them, I just look at them through my eyes. The mountains send us an invitation for silent contemplation.

Emerson was a Nature lover. When I read his words, I can feel his love for it. It's like me talking about it, but in a poetic way. I can hear the tone of his heart. Huachuma is the key to that real place within you, the heart consciousness, a lively field full of grass, fresh water and sunshine. It's what the Sufis called the knowledge of the heart that can only be felt.

How incredible is the resonance between Hesse, Emerson and Rumi, a 13th century Sufi mystic who gifted the world with timeless, mystical poetry. Rumi placed intuition above

The Cactus of Sanity

intellect and reason. Reading Rumi is like talking to a grandfather who lived a long, fulfilling life. German, American and Persian, centuries and oceans apart, speaking about the same thing. And there are others whom I respect and love but did not mention. All these people have expressed themselves and shared their inner world. These were the truth seekers.

CHAPTER 7

MEETING PATRICK SWAYZE IN THE BATHROOM: HOLLYWOOD ENCOUNTERS HUACHUMA

My first wife and I took a trip to New York somewhere between 2001 and 2004. I was excited to get out of the cult environment where both she and I were living in California. It just was a nice break.

New York was noisy. In the relatively short time I spent in Northern California by then, living in a pine forest, I came to love the peace and silence of Nature. In fact, I had loved it all my life, but I had never actually lived in it. But, since I was born in a city and lived in cities all my life before I moved to Peru in April 2009, I was fine to handle the city of New York. It just wasn't my preference anymore.

Among different things we did, my wife wanted us to go see *The Lion King*, a Broadway show. I didn't mind, although theater never was my thing. I preferred movies. My excitement was ignited when she said that Patrick Swayze was performing in it. This changed my mood. Patrick Swayze was an actor I liked after watching *Ghost* many times in my

The Cactus of Sanity

youth, a beautiful love story. It reminded me of one of my childhood obsessions with trying to move objects with my mind, which I never developed but always wanted to. I remember spending hours trying to move a box of matches with my thoughts when I was about 5 years old. This movie ignited the old wish. So, to see Patrick Swayze in real life was something I wanted to do.

We had good seats, just a few rows from the stage, and I could see Patrick Swayze and the other actors well. I liked watching him perform. He seemed to be enjoying himself on the stage even more than in the movie. He truly was a dancer. After the performance we went to have dinner in a nearby restaurant my wife had recommended. I was surprised to find out Patrick Swayze was having dinner there too. It felt good to be sharing the same space with a celebrity whom I actually liked. I even thought about going to his table and asking for an autograph, but I didn't want to be rude and invade his privacy.

Sometime during dinner, I excused myself and went to the bathroom. After washing my hands I stepped out and stumbled upon a man in the bathroom doorway. It was Patrick. We just looked one another in the eyes for a second. He had a peaceful and friendly look. We both kept moving after a little pause. When I came to my table I told my wife that I just met Patrick Swayze in the bathroom. She asked me if I talked to him. I said no, we just looked at one another. I could have just said, "Hi, Patrick, you are a good dancer and I enjoyed your performance," but I didn't.

When we left the restaurant, we took a walk down Broadway. I kept rewinding our meeting with Patrick in my head. I never shared this story until now. I didn't think it was important. I never liked seeing people cheering for celebrities. I always thought it was foolish. You wouldn't see me in this crowd. But with Patrick it felt different. From that one moment I looked at his eyes, I felt like he was a humble, simple and real person. I liked that about him. Another 15 years passed before I had the opportunity to enter Hollywood myself, not as someone's fan but as a film director.

During a Huachuma ceremony in 2017, I had the idea of bringing my ideas onto a screen, small or big, didn't matter. I thought that people would feel a visual interaction more personally and deeply. Perhaps it was the first time I thought of making a film about the healing work I do with Huachuma medicine in Peru. Interestingly enough, during that time, some of our guests had a family member who was well connected with prominent Hollywood producers. They told me she was

The Cactus of Sanity

even friends with James Cameron! After sharing my ideas with them, they said that they would talk to her and see if this were something she would like to do. I felt excited by the prospect of working with James Cameron, creating films like *Avatar* while injecting more shamanic ideas into the collective consciousness and thus facilitating a worldwide spiritual awakening.

A while later, that person came to Peru. I will only use the first letter of her first name to respect her privacy, even though she has recently passed away. Being too busy, P. only came for one week and we had three ceremonies, during which I shared with her my vision. She seemed to be interested and said that she would be back. Before she left, I asked her if she could give a copy of my book, *PATH: Seeking Truth in a World of Lies*, to James Cameron, with whom she met frequently on business and social events. She had shown me pictures on her phone of her being with him. She said that John Cameron was involved in James's films as a co-producer, and it would be right to express my admiration to him as well. She also knew Stephen King, whose books I read a long time ago, and Buzz Aldrin, the astronaut who walked on the moon, who was a guest at her house during one of our Skype calls. I was very excited to get to know these people and ask them personal questions. When she asked me what I wanted to ask Buzz Aldrin, whether he saw aliens on the Moon or if the Earth were flat, I laughed and said no, I just want to ask him how it feels to look at Earth from space, being so far away from home. She said it could be arranged.

I wrote two cards and included one in each copy of my book to James and John Cameron. I really wanted them to read it and see if the content could get on a screen. I love my books, they are written from a place of truth-seeking and, I believe, can be useful for many people who are searching for their path. I felt that bringing my ideas to a screen would affect the world in a positive way. I saw Hollywood as a "world speaker." If used wisely, it could make a difference in the way people think and feel about life, love, peace and healing via plant medicine, which is a necessity in a rapidly changing world. I felt like people needed good, hopeful, real messages to balance the endless car chasing, bank robberies and violence often seen in movies.

I thought delivering my message through this world speaker could inspire people toward personal change that eventually would positively affect the collective. I was certain that if I were given a chance to introduce politicians to Huachuma, once being awakened to the beauty of Nature and the amazing soul healing that follows the experience, they would speak in her defense and allow an intelligent debate about the prohibition on sacred plants to begin. We need a sensible dialog supported by facts in order to change the legislation against nature that exists currently. The *U.S. Controlled Substances Act* puts mescaline with heroin as a Schedule 1 drug, described as unsafe, having a high potential for abuse and no accredited medical use. All three statements are false when it comes to mescaline. I wanted to correct this. An ambitious project but so what? Life is ambitious. If a fragile blade of grass can break through solid concrete and push through asphalt on its way to light, why can't we break through legislation that is based on false data on our path toward personal healing and expansion of consciousness?

We kept in touch when she left back to California. After a while she wrote me saying that she was coming back next year with a cameraman. I was very excited and couldn't believe this was actually happening. I could reach the world with the message of healing via plant medicine, preservation of Nature and its gifts to humanity, and the importance of changing the way we live if we all want to have a future. I didn't even need to prepare for it. I knew exactly where to film and what to say. I was more than ready; I was impatient.

She came with a cameraman late in March, 2018. I took them to the most beautiful places around where we live, did ceremonies there, and filmed in real time. We did my interview for the film as well. Everything was ready to go. The footage was in the can, as the cameraman put it. But at the last ceremony there was an incident that changed the course of events and led to the cancelation of the project.

We did that last ceremony higher up in the mountains at the Eagle's Nest, a powerful ancient ceremonial site. As usual, we began at the lake nearby, and then, at the peak of the ceremony, we moved towards the ruins. This is one of my favorite places around here, so I wanted to include it in the film.

The Cactus of Sanity

We had about 12 people in the group at this time. One of the participants was a person who came to us with severe depression and suicidal tendencies. He stayed with us two months prior to it and was working through his process. He was triggered at the Eagle's Nest by the flying drone we used to capture the beauty of the place from the air. Upon returning home that day, when we stepped out of the cars and were about to enter the gate, he came to me and said that he was losing his mind and needed help. I said, OK, let's get inside, and I will take care of you. I felt he was sincere rather than craving attention, but even if he wasn't, considering his psychological history, I had to take his request seriously and treat him with utmost care. Upon entering the maloca, our ceremonial space, I did a tobacco cleansing ritual on him to help him calm down. He acted a bit dramatic and made unpleasant sounds. From the outside, it looked like an exorcism was being performed. Once he calmed down, I kept to the routine and closed the ceremony as we always do. I cannot close the ceremony until all participants are calm. No one can be left outside the protective circle.

This apparently was too much for P. to take. After the closing, she left the ceremonial space with anger. The next morning she called me and accused me of not working with integrity, when in fact, working with integrity is all I did last night. If integrity wasn't a factor, I would have ignored the guy and focused on filming the ending of the ceremony, thinking what would be the best for me. She accused me of not warning her that this was about to happen so she could leave the circle earlier. First of all, I couldn't tell a guy who says he is losing his mind to sit outside on a bench and wait until we film the closing of the ceremony before I could take care of him. I had to act accordingly and make sure he was back to his senses as soon as possible. And second, I didn't know that he would be so expressive. In any case, the door was open, and she or anyone else could have stepped out.

Although I disagreed with accusations, I understood her feelings and suggested that she come for the next day's ceremony, where we could talk about the situation in a good way. She agreed. But apparently, giving up on negativity was too much for P. to do and when she came the next day for the ceremony, she didn't even say hello to me when she stepped through the door. When we came to the river, our usual ceremonial spot, I observed her holding on to her negativity. I felt like she was expecting an apology, but I had done nothing to apologize for. I still made an attempt to help her release her anger, but she kept holding on to it. We didn't talk more that

The Cactus of Sanity

day, and after this ceremony she left and pulled the cameraman out of our center. The project was cancelled. We exchanged a few emails afterward, which carried the same energy.

I felt devastated. The greatest opportunity I had so far in my life was lost. Meeting James and John Cameron, Stephen King, Buzz Aldrin and other interesting people was no longer possible. I would no longer be invited to hold discreet Huachuma retreats for influential people in Santa Monica, California and Aspen, Colorado, and be the voice for change. The Hollywood fiasco felt like a loss of a great opportunity to do something big in my life and leave my humble impression in the course of history. But on the other hand, I felt stronger following my principles.

Two years have now passed, and I still sometimes wonder if playing along would have been wiser. This event created tension with the family members who invited her to come to Peru. My friendship with them was also broken. I still hoped one day to hear from John Cameron, who, she said, read my first book. She also said it wasn't easy to give it to his brother James. I thought maybe it had to do with copyrights and content issues. Later I heard the sad news that P. had died from lung cancer. I felt sorry for her and her family.

In order to heal this wound, I thought I needed to make my own films. I wanted to make documentaries to show how we work with the medicine in Peru and the stunning beauty of the surrounding nature. Operating on a tiny, personal budget, of course, would be much lesser in scale and seen on a much smaller screen; nevertheless, it would be my production, expressing what I feel. The first film I made I called *Divine Cactus*, which I sent to many film festivals. Some took it for screening but it didn't get any further. Since then, I have recycled the content, expanded on it and turned into another film called *The Cure*. Both of them are available on YouTube. (If you would like to watch them, you can find a direct link on my website, https://www.huachumawasi.com/)

When I was writing this chapter, my wife came to kiss me. I told her that I was writing this story and asked her how she feels today about the situation. "If you had behaved differently, it wouldn't be you. You are not a hypocrite," she said. This was reassuring. Apart from her external beauty, my wife is also so grounded and real. She is always one and the same person: loyal, reliable and receptive. Who knows how things would turn out if I were able to get into Hollywood. If I lost my family on the way to success, it would be a failure regardless of what could be achieved.

PART II

THE CACTUS OF SANITY

CHAPTER 8

HUACHUMA, THE HEALING VISIONARY CACTUS FROM PERU

In *The Mescaline Confession: Breaking through the Walls of Delusion*, I write about mescaline, the active alkaloid of Huachuma cactus. Among other things, I explore the scientific research conducted on mescaline during the first

The Cactus of Sanity

half of the 20th century. To avoid a repetition in this book, I would only like to summarize the subject matter for a new reader.

Huachuma is the original name given to the various mescaline-containing columnar cacti native to the Andes and used traditionally for millennia in Peru for healing and divination. The cactus thrives at around 3,000 meters (10,000 feet) above sea level and flowers beautifully between October and March, giving the lucky observer a gentle scent. Its flower opens for just one day and closes over the next two days. After this, the flower gradually dries out and forms a cocoon with new life-seeking seeds. Then, when ripe and ready, the cocoon pops and releases the seeds to the will of the wind. Thus the new life begins.

The most commonly used botanical names are Echinopsis Pachanoi (spineless) and Echinopsis Peruviana (with spine), but these names, of course, are only a shadow of the real essence of the plant, which is spiritual, not verbal. To realize this, it takes more than knowing the plant's name; it takes an experience that floats like a cloud beyond the horizon of botanical study.

"San Pedro" is the post-colonial name given to the psychoactive Andean cactus known by different names.

Sergey Baranov

"Huachuma" is the old Qechua name, which means "vision" or "that which makes one drunk." It is a visionary cactus with an amazing potential for healing. Seeing the world through its "eyes" is like being born again, but this time consciously.

With the invasion of the Spaniards in the early 16th century, native shamanic traditions of Peru faced the very real threat of extinction. The brutal intolerance of the Catholic Church would only allow for obedience and conversion, and certainly not "paganism" and "devil-worshipping" practices, as it generally viewed them.

How exactly some of these ancient traditions survived, nobody knows, but I have been entertaining the following thought: There could have potentially been a deal made — the natives could continue their use of their sacraments while worshiping Christian Saints. Saint Peter was an apostle who, according to Christian theology, received the keys to Heaven from Jesus Christ. A visual representation of this biblical scene can be found in an early Renaissance painting by Marco Zoppo (1468) depicting the saint holding the Keys of Heaven.

A parallel can be drawn between Zoppo's painting and an ancient carving found in the temple of Chavin de Huantar in

Peru, an anthropomorphic image of a deity, half-man, half-jaguar, half eagle, who holds the sacred cactus in his hand as the key to the state of consciousness it represents. Despite being created three thousand years apart, the similarity of the symbolism is quite apparent.

Seeing the parallels between the heavenly experience of the Huachuma cactus and the apostolic story from the newly adopted faith would naturally lead them to choose this name. Perhaps this allowance from the Church was made out of mercy or as a favor-seeking gesture in the eyes of God and the indigenous population.

In a similar way, at the time of the Inca dynasty, the Qechua people hid their mummies inside the wooden statues of Christian saints during the Corpus Christi feast — an annual liturgical solemnity and celebration of the body of Christ. Thus, while on the surface they worshiped the Christian saints, they were in fact revering their own.

In any case, the tradition has survived until today, albeit, of course, in a syncretic form of religion. And although the cloak of Christian terminology was pulled over its lungs, it hasn't been suffocated and remains breathing, like the mountains around you when you see them under the influence of Huachuma medicine.

Sergey Baranov

My introduction to this ancient mystery in 2005 was nothing less than a life-changing event, a fact that has slowly revealed itself over time. Back then, I was a spiritual seeker, who intuitively knew that plant medicine shamanism held the key to a kind of knowledge that could not be found in books. This type of knowledge was experiential, not intellectual. I was not satisfied with reading about the experience; I wanted the experience. Led by a burning desire and a spiritual thirst that up until then had resulted mainly in disappointment, I was fortunate to find people in Peru who had practiced shamanism for many decades and were dedicated healers.

Shamanism was something I had been drawn to since my early childhood. But living under the Soviet regime, the prospect of engaging with it did not look hopeful. As a kid I perceived life as a miracle, and I wanted to keep this feeling forever onward. I didn't want to grow up believing that life is a process of collecting stuff and saving for retirement. This prospect seemed rather too bleak.

This introduction to an ancient path became a new starting point in my life. My urge was calmed. My thirst was satisfied and spiritual hunger fed. A path of self-discovery ahead was now opened to me with a friendly and welcoming gesture. I kept coming back to work with the same people for three and

The Cactus of Sanity

a half years before I made the decision to move to Peru in April 2009, after feeling the call to serve the sacred Huachuma medicine. Landing in the Sacred Valley in the Andes felt like coming home. I knew I wanted to build my new life here around the medicine. And like a cactus offshoot, I took roots in new land.

This, of course, did not come without a price, not in money but in terms of the fear of death, which had been my unwelcome friend since early childhood. I describe my near-death experience in Mexico while working with Huichol Indians and the sacred Peyote in detail in my first book. Fearing death and seeking self-fulfillment from an early age were significant factors in the formation of my spiritual quest. This quest led me eventually to shamanism in Peru, where sacred medicinal plants were not only legal, but embedded in the culture, reaching back as far as the dawn of history. Coming to it with my own spiritual baggage, which mainly consisted of reading Eastern philosophies and contemplating them using psychedelics, was a good thing. I had a context and a "fertile ground" in which the seeds of new teaching from the mescaline-containing cactus could take root.

But even though my love for wisdom and a search for answers for life-long questions were my early allies, I could not have suspected how deep the "jaguar hole" actually goes. I can still remember the excitement I felt when I realized that plant-based shamanism was "the real deal" — an authentic path that actually works and is open to those who are unsatisfied with others' verbal descriptions of higher states of consciousness and are willing to step beyond their fear of the unknown.

Why bother? Why would we need this kind of experience in our lives? Why would we pay for this with the fears we cherish? Well, simply put, knowing this reality brings the happiness and joy of understanding. That's really it. There are no more rewards I'm after. Waking up in the morning with a peaceful, clear mind and gratitude for another day in my life is a generous gift I am infinitely thankful for.

The world that I've seen through the light of the sacred cactus was beyond belief. Its self-evident truth did not require one. Thus the shamanic perspective has simply become my new outlook. Although it is a very broad name given to diverse practices of healing, in fact, it is a way of living and interacting with the world. Not all of them include the use of psychoactive plants. In Siberia, for example, the invocation of ancestral spirits for the purpose of healing is normally achieved without using plants. For myself, however, this aspect of shamanism was not of such great interest. I was after an altered state of consciousness in which, I hoped, I could perceive the world in a different way, learning and spiritually growing from it, directly and experientially. In fact, a couple of years ago, I, myself, was responsible for introducing Siberian shamans to Huachuma. I gave my medicine to a person who was going to Altai, a region in Russia that has preserved its ancient shamanic tradition. After finishing his Huachuma retreat with us in Peru, he carried my medicine to the distant land of my ancestors. He reported back that the shamans he met were sending me their gratitude for the experience they had with my medicine. They said that the connection they made with Mother Nature was deeper than ever. The shamans, who lived in and worshiped Nature all their lives, found Huachuma cactus to reveal a new dimension. It's hard to beat such feedback! Siberian shamans do have a tradition of working with *Amanita Muscaria* mushrooms but it is less frequent today.

It's difficult to describe the feeling when, after a long search, a person finds a path that is actually fulfilling. And this is what the sacred cactus means to me: an oasis full of spring water in the middle of a desert, upon drinking from which, one realizes it is not a mirage.

Mescaline can easily lift you above your system of beliefs and allow you to perceive reality clearly. It opens your inner vision and helps you to see beyond religious dogma, scientific narrative, political objectives and social constructs. Free from ideology and dogma, the ancient path remains intact and clearly drawn on the map of consciousness. The daily miracle of Nature, which gets neglected in modern life, is recognized and worshipped with tears of gratitude. The healing energy of the sacred cactus is drunk like nectar with the beak of our soul. A light brighter than daylight is finally seen with the inner eyes and loved for its purity and beauty. A sense of belonging to a greater unity becomes a fact, not wishful thinking. Denying the physical world, which is sometimes needed at the early stages of a spiritual path in order to understand the difference, turns into acceptance, and living is seen as a service to a greater cause.

I think that each of us come to this world with this light, which then somehow vanishes under the sociocultural pressure during the process of growing up. Losing it causes fear and anxiety and eventually turns into depression, which

The Cactus of Sanity

is only a symptom of this separation from oneself. We feel alone and lonely, separated from the source of life, when, in fact, we are the leaves and flowers of the tree of life.

Reconnecting to our spiritual roots is "coming home," not in a hyperspace or separate reality surrounded by other beings, but here and now, in our familiar, known space, which becomes sacred the moment it is recognized as such. Huachuma is a beauty that cannot be conveyed but can be experienced.

CHAPTER 9

HUACHUMA'S PLACE IN HISTORY

When we understand human history and our evolutionary processes, it is clear that the core shamanic tradition worldwide is rooted in plants, just as plants are rooted in the earth. This is our connection to the Pachamama, Mother Earth, which has been severed by religious dogmatism over the last few thousand years in the West and East. Ancient India was shamanic. Vedic texts praise Soma. The ancient Bon tradition of Tibet was shamanic, then the Buddhists took over. Soma, the fly agaric mushroom, ephedra, iboga of Africa, Syrian rue, cannabis of the Middle East and other plants of the Old World were all used as shamanic tools to reach altered states of consciousness. Peyote, Huachuma, Ayahuasca, psilocybin mushrooms, Morning Glory seeds and other plant teachers and allies of North and South America were and still are used for healing today in the New World. These are facts of history, not assumptions or theories.

The term shaman comes from Siberia and means "healer." Siberian shamanism was nearly destroyed by the Soviet anti-religious repression in the 1930s. But political oppression is not the only reason for the eradication of shamanic cultures.

The Cactus of Sanity

Climate change, which can transform a botanical landscape, can also contribute to the loss of ancient knowledge. In any case, the ancient shamanic tradition of South America has survived aggressive religious suppression and persecution and has reached us in a living form that allows for direct experience.

Unfortunately, many other places have suffered tremendous cultural losses over the centuries and were able to preserve their shamanic tradition only in the form of folklore. Although that may be sufficient to maintain its identity and historical presence, this type of shamanism has lost its power to heal and guide people on their paths. No amount of drumming will provide you with the clarity you need to see and understand yourself. No matter how many myths you hear, they will never teach you living wisdom. No matter how many legends are told over and over again, they will not have the power to transform your life. All this is interesting but remains in the realm of concepts. Superficial should not be confused with the supernatural.

I address the historical importance of Huachuma for the people of Peru and the whole South American continent in *The Mescaline Confession*. Here I would only like to add that it is increasingly clear that Nature is on the side of humanity and always has been. Why do I bring this up? Because today, we hear that the Pope says that COVID-19 is Nature's response to its abuse by humans. This notion is so absurd that it must be called out.

There are two aspects that need to be explained. First is the fact that the Catholic Church and its doctrines are in essence anti-Nature. In *The Mescaline Confession* I go deeper into the relationship between plants and the Catholic Church, which viewed them as being the Devil's roots. Thus, the people who cured others using plants were viewed as sorcerers who needed to die horrible deaths. This is the actual history of the Catholic Church in the 16th century that sponsored the brutal conquest of the peoples of South and North America. Never in nearly 2000 years of Christianity was Nature worshipped; rather, it was denigrated and rejected as devilish forces. So, for someone who knows history, the notion that Nature is revered by the Pope is laughable.

Second, speaking from my own experience working with sacred plants for 15 years and serving Huachuma for 11 as I write these words, I can say that Nature is on our side. Nature is a loving parent, unlike the vengeful Christian God, who, we are told, is loving and merciful and yet cursed Adam and Eve, his only children, for eternity and expelled them from the Garden of Eden for mere childish disobedience. Nature is the center of shamanic traditions all over the world. It's a source of healing for people who call it Mother, not those who see the Devil hiding in the plants. Of course, if you keep excavating a mountain for building material, causing a part of it to collapse and kill workers, the blame is yours, not Nature's. It's just physics, not spiritual vengeance. COVID-19 is a virus that has a destructive purpose. To say that coronavirus is Nature's vengeance on humanity is like saying that all wars, starvation and disease since time immemorial all came from Nature trying to get rid of humanity. Nature loves us as we love Nature. This is the basic principle of shamanism, the very same principle that got many people killed during the Spanish conquest of America. It is important to discern politics from true spirituality, and true spirituality comes from the heart.

Plant teachers are the gateway to the world of Spirit, where healing and guidance are found. Plant medicine is a tool that can easily bypass words, concepts and belief systems — all of which, at best, can serve as road signs and, at worst, as gatekeepers. This is why sacred plants are feared and have been suppressed. They expand consciousness and democratize individual divine connection. They open up your doors of perception and allow you to stare at yourself and the Universe with fresh and unbiased eyes. This is where you find an abundance of healing energy, as full of insights as the ocean is full of fish. And this ocean is neutral waters, where you can fish with your mind all you want. No one owns it. Dare to enter and claim your place in the Cosmos. Responsible use of psychoactive plants is the rope we can use to pull ourselves out of the quagmire of materialism and the mess we have collectively created as modern humans. It is a great cultural mistake to label sacred medicines as drugs. This derogatory and ignorant view must be replaced with the truth.

We have to return to Nature. But that doesn't mean that we have to abandon our homes and build huts made of branches. This is just another extreme. A return to Nature means opening our hearts and minds to intuitive learning from plants, which truly are the greatest and oldest teachers of humanity. With their help we find a place within where we can think clearly and feel deeply. The ability to see inside yourself objectively and honestly brings healing and change. A sincere wish to understand yourself and your place in the Universe is where the spiritual search begins. But other components are required in order to complete the puzzle.

Attaining higher states of consciousness is achievable under certain conditions. This is exactly why so many people are falling into ideologies that are supposed to help them to reach

The Cactus of Sanity

this state of being. Unfortunately, many who are forced to cross a spiritual desert to find the oasis of life never see this utopian landscape. With the help of sacred plants and certain guidance, this oasis is not only revealed on the map of consciousness but is given a physical address.

For me, this is working with sacred plants, the Huachuma cactus in particular. To you, it may be something else. It's up to you to judge whether or not it works. Speaking for myself, I found Huachuma to be the most amazing spiritual medicine on our planet. Its compatibility with our physiology and psychology is simply stunning. Next to it, I would consider DMT, the active alkaloid found in the Chacruna leaves that are added to the Ayahuasca brew in a traditional preparation. It is for those who are in a hurry. But taking a fast track route to cosmic awakening might not be the best way for you to get there, because landing back in reality can be pretty rough. Mescaline is interesting in the way that it both connects you to a higher consciousness and mystical realms of existence, but at the same time it provides you with a safe return to your waking consciousness. This is a very profound and grounding experience. This is why we recommend partaking in Huachuma after Ayahuasca. Huachuma is a highly effective way of bridging the gap between realities. It can ensure that your sanity remains intact upon arriving back in the city, where you might find yourself sitting in Starbucks talking to aliens while having your cappuccino. We can speculate and debate as to how this medicine should be administered, but more important is to do it in a way that works. Rather than sacrificing animals and humans to appease the gods, we sacrifice our fears to appease ourselves. Our objective is to restore balance within and outside of us, taking a gentle but firm approach that delivers life-changing results. I call it "surfing through ignorance on the back of a Huachuma cactus."

We are the caretakers of the Earth but we have lost our path. Nature is trying to wake us up from a trance to remind us that we are a part of it, and it's time to return home. Opening up to humanity on a large scale in the last 20 years by offering its gifts in the form of plant medicine, Nature shows its intent to collaborate by giving us an open hand, not a fist. It helps to wake us up from our self-destructive sleep. It is a gesture of love, not an act of violence and destruction. This is what I feel working with the sacred Huachuma cactus.

If you are already working with plant medicines but aren't seeing results manifesting in your life, then something isn't quite right. The medicine, however, is not to blame. It is a tool the Earth offers us, and, like any tool, it can be used in more

The Cactus of Sanity

and less effective ways. For our part at Huachuma Wasi, it takes experience and knowledge of medicine to guide the process, and for your part as a guest, it takes commitment to receive it. It takes two to tango. Just as there are many layers to the clouds, you, too, have many layers that the medicine can help you to understand. Just as the sunlight illuminates the clouds so that we can see them, Huachuma illuminates your consciousness so that you become aware of it.

We are living in a critical time in which an awakening has become a necessity for the many, not a privilege for the few. If we do not wake up now, we might soon not have a world to wake up to. Although no one owes us salvation from our own ignorance, the generosity of Nature is immense, and it welcomes those who are willing to learn from it. In this era of information, ignorance is a choice. We may remain asleep to all the madness we see in the world, or we can take responsibility for our lives and together try to make a difference. Only we are responsible for our happiness and well-being. The future of the world is in our hands.

CHAPTER 10

HUACHUMA, THE UNFORGETTABLE MYSTERY

"The most beautiful thing we can experience is the mysterious; it is the source of all true art and science."

— Albert Einstein

Many times I have been asked what is the most important thing I've learned from working with Huachuma medicine over the years. Not once I could answer it simply, although I always did it truthfully.

This is not because I didn't have something to say. In fact, I had a lot to say, perhaps even too much, which created an obstacle for a simple answer. If you ask me this question today, I don't think much has changed. I would still not know where to start and where to end. But regardless of how truthful my words are, they are not capable of reflecting the experience. They can only point the way.

We all have heard about the Tree of Life and Tree of Knowledge, two magical trees that supposedly grew in the Garden of Eden, the latter of which being responsible for the Fall of humanity after Eve ate an apple from it. Bypassing the moral side of the story, which can be debated, I would like to make the following point. It has been imprinted in our Western minds that anything magical or miraculous is either a myth found in a children's story or written in the Bible. What if I told you that magic is found right here and now on Earth? Not the magic you see on the stage performed by David Copperfield, who is perhaps the greatest illusionist of our time, but the magic that is capable of actually transforming your life. Watching Copperfield fly off the stage is entertaining but does not change anything in your life.

For me, magic has a different meaning. It's the magic of healing and feeling, the alchemical process during which your ego melts and, out of this psychic lava, your true self appears. It can melt the parts of your soul that were frozen by trauma and give you your life back, a life of joy, clarity, confidence and strength. It has the power to recalibrate your brain chemistry and permanently fix the imbalances, thus healing depression, anxiety and fear. It has the power to reset you and give you a fresh start in life. This is what, with proper guidance, sacred plants can do. They can free your mind so you can fly above ideologies and belief systems. That's the kind of flight you would want to book a seat on. This is what I call magic.

When I heard about the Tree of Life and the Tree of Knowledge in the Biblical story, I was fascinated. I thought that those kinds of trees must be found somewhere on Earth, otherwise it would torture our hearts and minds to hear about them without the possibility of ever reaching them. Decades later, I was led to sacred plants in South and North America, and thus a journey of self-discovery has taken on a new meaning. Today, I have many Huachuma cacti growing in my garden. Sustaining my soul by harvesting from my garden keeps me clear and straight on my path. No need for Heaven, no fear of the Devil. All is good and everyone is happy. Huachuma, like a few other sacred plants such as Peyote and Ayahuasca, is here to serve humanity, to guide it through the darkness that we have imposed on ourselves. It's a medicine that enlightens us so we can see our path with clarity and understanding. I touch upon this subject, *The Mescaline Confession: Breaking through the Walls of Delusion*, a book that was endorsed by Graham Hancock, a best-selling author, who has reviewed it and said that "is a thought-provoking, heartfelt, informative and above all important

The Cactus of Sanity

book. Highly recommended to anyone who feels that things are not as they should be in the world today. "

Everyone finds his or her own truth and bases their lives upon it. It may not resonate with the ideas expressed by the greatest minds known to human history. This, however, should not set you back on your path of self-discovery. Each of us has our own path to walk, our own lessons to learn and our own wisdom to find. Yet we enhance our human experience when we all share the understanding that truth can only be realized for oneself, and words are not the things for which they stand. Many ancient teachings support this claim.

"What is the ultimate teaching of Buddhism? You won't understand it until you have it," says Shitou Xiqian, an 8th-century Zen Buddhist teacher.

The Diamond Sutra states, "What is known of the teaching of Buddha is not the teaching of Buddha."

The Lankavatara Sutra says, "With the lamp of the word and discrimination one must go beyond the word and discrimination and enter upon the path of realization."

Each of these statements points to the necessity of having an immediate spiritual experience to know the truth.

And one more, from Rumi: "Can I explain the Friend to one for whom he is not a Friend?" Of course not! You just can't. You can only inspire him to find his own connection through which he will know the Friend firsthand.

The point here is that someone's truth is not your truth unless you realize it for yourself and, thus, it becomes you. From this perspective, guidance is important but following it blindly does not serve you well. Words are only the symbols on the map of consciousness. They are the road signs that point the direction that a seeker of truth must take.

The problem with any religious and spiritual teaching is that the teachers had to use language to convey the teaching. Language is a tool used in time to try to describe a timeless experience — what I would call the Divine presence. The history of all religions is similar in one important respect. In every religion there were enlightened people who not only spoke the truth but themselves were the truth. However, these individuals were a few among the many. The majority were students of words about the truth, not students of the truth itself. Although the words are indispensable in pointing the way, at the same time they can become a mind trap that holds us captive. Thus dogma is born.

The Cactus of Sanity

We learn by firsthand experience, not by other people's description of it. To become a painter, you have to paint; to become a musician you have to play an instrument; to become a chef you have to cook; to become a driver you have to drive. How can this be different in learning about the spiritual nature of reality? This crucial point must be cemented in one's understanding.

But this is not at all to say that the saints and spiritual teachers of humanity wasted their time. Without them, we wouldn't even have a sense of direction beyond our instinctive mode of living. Many of us are still living that way regardless. The greatest and brightest among us have paved the way forward. However, if we become obsessed with words and take them literally, we are running the risk of losing ourselves in the labyrinths of the mind.

Nor should we ignore words altogether, which would lead to another extreme. I find the middle way to be the most productive. "Learning but discerning" is my personal motto. It has proven to work in my own experience. Whatever I read, I test with my own ability to perceive and understand. If theology taught discernment I would consider taking a class. But what is theology if not a mystical insight that has been rationalized in terms of general knowledge? The founders of any religion were mystics first, then theologians. It follows that the mystical experience, firsthand spiritual knowledge, is what we should be seeking.

I touch on this subject in my first book. Religion is a natural science that should be guided by experience, just as physical science is guided by research. This leads me back to the method of discernment I talked about earlier: a plant-based shamanic experience that can enlighten you to the point of crystal clarity, in which you are able to separate the wheat from the chaff. The shamanic landscape is vast and not all of its aspects lead to this end. However, I found mescaline-containing cacti like Peyote of Mexico and Huachuma of Peru to be the ones that do. It is up to you to discover for yourself that the path of realization is intuitive, not verbal.

Even when we try to describe something simple as grass to another person, we only can say that it is green. However, the experience of seeing green grass is much more than a description. Being so limited in our communicative abilities when it comes to even describing a visible object, how much more limited and less capable are we when we try to describe a personal, spiritual experience? When I think about it, I can feel the pain of all those Sufis, saints and real teachers who

The Cactus of Sanity

felt like victims of their own words. And yet, they tried their very best to convey to us the glory of Divine reality.

To me, salvation means to touch the heart of existence and know it by experience. To seek salvation in words is like trying to cross an ocean by looking at the map. Today any map is available, yet still, it takes action to reach a destination.

CHAPTER 11

THE HEALING BEAUTY OF HUACHUMA

Huachuma healing is deep and lasting. Personally, I do not focus on the physical side. I believe that the physical is a reflection of the spiritual, therefore the spiritual side of yourself is where the focus should be. When we heal our spirit, the body responds by healing itself. The body is a great healer but it has to be given a chance to do its job. Think of it as a cut on your skin that will not heal if you scratch it daily. You have to leave your scratch alone to heal. A similar process is happening within our minds. Our spirit needs to be given the time to heal its wounds. Stress, as much as fear, is a killer. Stress is that scratching of the wound that does not allow for healing. Constant stress is a poison for the body and mind.

One thing that Huachuma does is relaxes you to a point of serenity when your body, mind and spirit all find deep rest. Recovery happens during this time. It is a great restorer of balance, healing and vitality. It resets you. Just as you reboot your computer when it freezes, in the same way Huachuma reboots you when you get frozen by stress, fear, anxiety and depression. Somehow it has an ability to recalibrate your brain chemistry to its proper balance, which results in a lasting feeling of well-being. I don't know the science of it, I can only say how I feel it works. Huachuma has a direct impact on your central nervous system and brain. You can literally feel it there, as though you allowed a healing spirit to enter your body and fix you up. This not to be confused with silly Hollywood movies when people get possessed by demons and act mindlessly. When you take Huachuma, you remain you, but a better you, the you that is awake. You radiate love and joy, and it shows on your face. Here, I am reminded of one of Rumi's poems, which asks the question: Does happiness reflect in your face from the wine of the true religion? It certainly does with Huachuma.

It also connects you deeply to Nature and allows natural sounds to advance the healing. Lying on the grass and listening to birds for hours has an incredibly deep healing effect. Listening to the wind playing with leaves and the sound of water flowing nearby brings you to tears of happiness. You literally feel like you have been nurtured by your loving mother. This deeply profound healing experience resurrects you from "sleep walking" into real living. It releases all stress and allows your body, mind and spirit to heal. You feel like you are drawing healing energy from the sun, from the birds, from the trees, from the grass from the water, from the land. You restore your vitality to maximum and after just a few weeks you are ready to go home and live a better life. The experience remains in Peru, but the connection that you have made with yourself and Nature here comes with you. You can recall it at will and dwell in its presence. The deeper the connection made during the work, the longer it'll stay with you.

It has many levels too. In small doses it is purely therapeutic, a mood modulator, relaxant and antidepressant. A medium dose is both therapeutic and creative. And in high doses it is therapeutic and mystical. The way I work with people is in a gradual, personalized way. I adjust medicine to each person according to what I feel that person needs at the time. Then, slowly, together we go deeper until the person is finding confidence in him or herself and the medicine that allows it to move deeper. I can have new and experienced people in the same group, and all will reach a place of healing, beauty and joy, in their own pace. I've seen many people over the years who come with an idea of healing, but when they find real healing, they are so grateful and amazed. Huachuma awakens you to the beauty of Nature, to which you respond with love. This feeling of gratitude and love is the healer. It shows you around so you can appreciate and express gratitude.

The healing power of Huachuma is amplified by the mountains, its natural habitat, its home. It makes you see them

The Cactus of Sanity

with so much more beauty. There is something about the mountains I never knew in my life. I was born in a city and lived in three countries before I moved to the Andes of Peru. And even though I love all of Nature's expressions, mountains have struck me most. I've taken Huachuma in the rainforest, I've had it in a desert, and I've drunk it near the ocean. Each place has its own beauty and lessons. However, doing it in the mountains, in its home, is a different feeling. Whatever depth you think you have reached by doing it elsewhere, mountains still offer more. Huachuma loves thin air and a view.

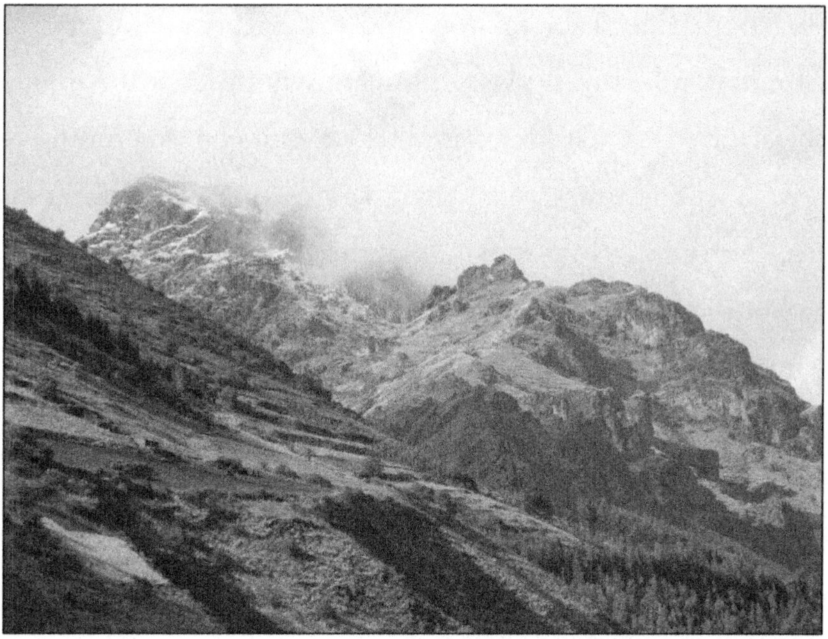

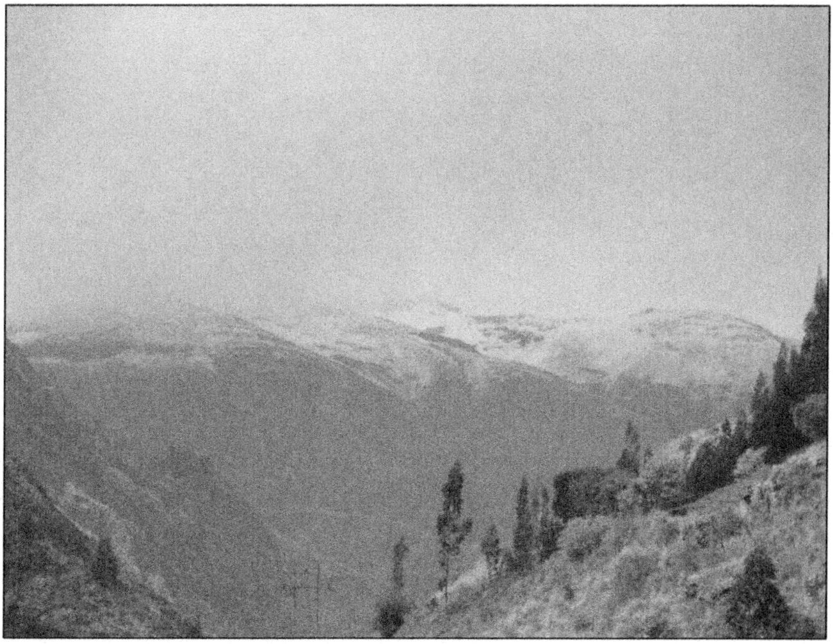

The Cactus of Sanity

Huachuma has a lot in store and can surprise you with its infinite depth. But it gives you what you need, which might not always be what you want. Like a guitar needs tuning to play music, it tunes you so you can play again. Huachuma gives everything but demands nothing. Its generosity comes without any requests. It doesn't ask you to keep a strict diet, refrain from sex, self-isolate. It allows you to eat whatever you want, to have intimacy, to socialize. Even more so, you feel like you want to do it yourself. You want to be a part of humanity, you want to embrace loving relationships, you want to enjoy food and good rest. It helps you to appreciate and enjoy your life more.

Huachuma is a pro-life medicine. It is a life healer.

CHAPTER 12

HUACHUMA IS THE LIQUID SUN

My previous book, *The Mescaline Confession*, has a chapter called, "Mescaline and the Sun." In it, I write about the spiritual significance of the Sun and the reverence with which ancient cultures regarded it. Here, I will share another aspect of this connection.

What do I feel when I take Huachuma? Well, the whole of creation, in fact. I feel the birth of the Universe. I feel the moment when light shines itself out of darkness and gives life. I feel the love for life with which this happened.

I feel, quite literally, as though I drink the sun. Huachuma cactus grows in the mountains, and sunlight is its main sustenance. It absorbs and converts light energy into food, which makes the cactus grow. Thus, we can say that the body of the cactus is the body of the sun. And we can say that it's the body of God as well, but this claim can be only substantiated through the experience. I can make you feel it, but I cannot tell you what it feels like.

This feeling explains why one can see so much light while under the influence of Huachuma. It can get so bright that you just cannot look at the clouds or even grass without feeling that you have been transported into a fairy tale. This blinding beauty is pleasantly shocking and lifts you above all the fears and pain you might have carried within you prior to it. It illuminates you and fills you up with love and confidence to live a better, healthier and happier life.

This is why at Huachuma Wasi, we conduct our ceremony in daylight, to absorb sunlight and heal ourselves with the beauty of Nature. Don't worry — we don't get cooked! We have plenty of shade under the trees. All is good in moderation and balance. Perhaps it would be the most beautiful and healing experience of your life. At least, this is how it feels to me.

There is one other aspect of this experience that I have uncovered over the years of working with Huachuma. It might sound a bit strange at first to hear that we, too, can process the sun's energy through photosynthesis and convert it to spiritual food. It's not a metaphor. I can actually feel myself growing during every ceremony I do. Like a muscle that breaks down during weightlifting and then the body repairs itself by adding more muscle tissue, I feel a similar process happening on a metaphysical level. Our consciousness gets stretched during a Huachuma experience. It expands during the ceremony and then allows the body to heal itself and gain the weight of understanding when we rest. This is why we do ceremonies every two days all year round, to balance the work and rest.

But the actual process of photosynthesis in humans can be experienced on a physical level. You can actually consume impressions like you consume food. The mechanism of this cannot be explained in words. It is experiential, like the Huachuma flower, which has an amazing scent that you can smell but not describe. You can also consume the sounds just like you drink water.

This is not to say that I don't eat normal food or drink water. Of course I do and find joy in doing so. We are built by Nature to eat and drink and this must be respected; like our sexuality, it's part of who we are. The process I speak of is metaphysical, one I find to be the engine of personal healing and spiritual growth.

Interestingly enough, G.I. Gurdjieff wrote about consuming impressions as a food for our higher centers; that is, the advanced faculties of the subtle body. But the problem is that even the best ideas he spoke about remained in the realm of theory. Without the actual experience, these are just words. A good analogy would be that the followers of the Fourth Way are mechanics who never exit the auto-shop. They know how the car is built and all its parts, they know how the engine works, but they never take a car for a ride. The fuel tank is empty. The Huachuma cactus is the fuel that gets you out of the garage and sets you on your journey. Only then, when you drive this car through the desert, feeling the wind on your face and the thrill of movement through the air, do you know what driving actually means.

I would like to share feedback from one of our guests, Kristen Yates, who actually described this process in her retreat journal without hearing this idea before:

FEAST OF LOVE

Over these past weeks working together with Sergey and Huachuma, the medicine has illuminated where I've needed healing, and taught me how to feel. My entire life, I thought I was feeling — but in truth, I was thinking about feeling. Always thinking... about... everything.

What does it truly mean to feel — without the thinking?

What does Huachuma have for me on this final day?

The leaves flicker and dance overhead, and I am transfixed by their language. Everything is so alive — it nearly overwhelms me. How are we not living constantly in awe, moving through a world that is so... alive?

I start to feel my inner child awaken, instantaneously clarifying for me things I'd forgotten. I see her in the dancing trees, hear her in the laughing river, feel her in the softness of the grass beneath me. She is an artist, a creator, so playful and loving and free. How have I forgotten that? When did I stop giving her permission to be who she is — a creator?

When did I stop trusting her innate, infinite creative path? She is here to play and explore — when did she become so caged in?

I'm struck with the knowledge that I've attached to men who embody their wounded child, as a connection for me back to mine. Immediately, this knowing is washed over by the powerful healing waters below, leaving me cleansed and renewed — completely connected to my blissful and infinitely wise and creative child within.

The river becomes me then, roaring through my blockages, relentlessly flowing from an infinite Source. Where does it come from? The answer is immediate. It is here. It is me. The Source of it all. It flows through me, cleansing me, and it is me. There is no beginning because it is a limitless outpouring of energy and potential... creativity and play.

I am overcome with the need to move now — to merge the earth with my feet, play in its vastness, drink the river's roar more deeply into my veins. I cross the trail to a flat rock perched above the river, and lay on its warm, smooth surface. Closing my eyes the vibrant paradise around me turns to an ecstatic kaleidoscope of its own behind my eyes.

Surrender. Show me. Teach me.

I become the river. She is me. I am her. Our infinite Source forever feeding new energy, new life, never-ending. It's so clear — this Source. Life doesn't begin, or end. Life — the Universe — IS.

It is the rushing river with an infinite wellspring leading to an infinite ocean of love and life forever.

There is "me", but also, there isn't... "me". There is no "me" separate from "that".

There is only...

I AM.

My eyes crack open slightly, turning to slivers, taking in an impossible brightness.

Suddenly, I am completely overtaken by beauty in a way I cannot describe.

To be transparent with you, I have no real words for this moment — the medicine is beyond human words.

One thing I've learned is that emotion and experience are at one energetic frequency, and words are at another, lower frequency. We need them, of course — but there are experiences which quite literally have no words to adequately depict them.

The magnificence of the Sacred Valley before me overwhelms me beyond belief – it becomes me. There is no "me" separate from this infinite beauty — heaven on earth.

I feel a sensation of being filled to the brim with this beauty — as though eating from a divine, never-ending Feast. The sensation is so overwhelming and filling, I nearly have to look away. But I'm transfixed.

Consuming hungrily with my eyes, ears, and body — it strikes me that I am eating a gluttonous feast with my senses, yet somehow, it never reaches the brim — and I don't need to feel guilty about it. I somehow have an endless capacity to take in this nourishment, merge with it, to "feast" with my eyes in this buffet of paradise. It's unbelievable.

I realize that I can now consume Nature in the same way that I consume food, only much more so. Just like our body produces energy out of food, our soul produces healing out of beauty. I now understand why Sergey conducts his ceremonies in the way he does. He understands that too. Be in Nature, see her, feel her, smell her,

The Cactus of Sanity

hear her, consume her. This message imprints into my cells, and somehow I know the gift of this beauty will not leave me once I leave Peru.

I am a part of it, I am that — infinite energy creating all of this beauty, it is me. We are literally one and the same. I can hardly believe it, and yet nothing has ever made more sense. Feasting on beauty here is simply returning home, nothing has ever been more right.

Tears of gratitude flood my eyes, turning the scene before me into a watery mosaic of heaven I never expected to experience while here on this Earth.

Back at my little grove in the forest, Sergey is waiting and smiling — I express to him this awe and amazement in realizing we literally feast with our eyes to consume the beauty that IS us.

He laughs knowingly, cactus-colored eyes sparkling, and says to me, "I want you to share this with the world."

On the way back we cross the river, and I stop to breathe in this magical place for one more time. Thank you, Mother Nature, thank you, Huachuma, thank you Sergey. Gratitude fills my soul in a way that defies words.

As we turn to follow the sunset home, infinite Source plunges relentlessly forth through her riverbanks, flooding my entirety with the Knowing and Beingness of her sacred love and Our infinite life, a new life, illuminated by this healing medicine.

She experienced what was only possible in theory to the Fourth Way.

To end this chapter, I want to share one therapeutic aspect of Huachuma that can be very useful for people who are sunlight deficient, especially those who live in the northern parts of the United States, Canada and Europe. These regions in which days are short and do not have much sun throughout the year cause depression in many people. The climatic source for this disorder is often ascribed to personal faults, which makes matters worse. Over the years working with people, I've had many guests from northern Europe who came here starving for sunlight, especially during the winter months in Europe. Being in sunny countries is healing in itself, but if travel is not possible, a therapeutic dose of Huachuma can help.

Huachuma has the amazing quality of extracting light from different objects. For example, by taking a small dose, you can extract light from a candle, which will feel like you are sitting by a fireplace. You can extract light from a flower. You can extract light from a rain cloud by simply looking at it. On a higher dose of Huachuma, you can even extract light from total

The Cactus of Sanity

darkness, for darkness also contains light that makes it visible. The Taoist yin/yang symbol comes to mind, but I digress.

The first time I heard about night vision in a shamanic context was in Mexico during my apprenticeship with Huichol Indians and peyote. While I was able actually to see in the dark like a nocturnal animal, I felt that, personally, what was more important was to apply this night vision to a spiritual darkness. I didn't mind using a flashlight while walking in the woods, but what I really wanted was to see into the darkness that has enslaved our world. To see into the shadows hidden behind intent, to see through deception and lies, to see through pretenses and fake smiles — I felt this type of vision was needed most.

I would recommend that people who suffer from Seasonal Affective Disorder (SAD) come visit us in Peru in October, when we still have lots of sunshine and plenty of Huachuma to help you to move through the winter months back home. This can help reduce the debilitating fatigue and depression caused by lack of sunlight without using antidepressants, which are addictive and can be harmful in the long run. The light therapy of Huachuma is both external and internal, something that cannot be achieved artificially. You can buy plenty of mechanical UV lights, which can be helpful living in a city, but they will not warm up your spirit. This light is superficial, and its therapeutic effects don't last long. Huachuma may compensate for the lack of sunlight exposure, which is important for sustaining mental health.

Huachuma helps reset the biorhythms responsible for sleeping and waking. It can help with insomnia as well, a sleep disorder that results in daytime sleepiness, irritability, fatigue and depression. Insomnia makes focusing and learning difficult, affects relationships and can cause car accidents. It's a very annoying condition that has a negative effect on our lives. Stress-induced insomnia can be worsened by lack of sunlight. Sleeping pills do not cure insomnia or reduce stress. They mask the underlying condition and, just like antidepressants, have a short-term effect with long term negative consequences. Huachuma does both, reduces stress and provides inner sunlight, thus recalibrating the biorhythms of the body. We start our ceremonies early in the day to catch the morning sun, which has a special quality to it. A few weeks of Huachuma therapy, which naturally includes light and sound therapy (the sounds of Nature) can last throughout the year and beyond. You can also learn how to maintain it.

This therapy is not only for people who suffer from SAD, but also for anyone who seeks relaxation, contemplation and clarity

The Cactus of Sanity

— all the ingredients of healing and well-being. Balance and restoration require a release of trapped negative emotions that block healing energy from circulation. Huachuma has taught me to draw healing energies from Nature like bees draw nectar from flowers to make honey. By doing this, I make spiritual honey: an ecstasy that results in a state of well-being.

CHAPTER 13

HUACHUMA AND THE THIRD EYE

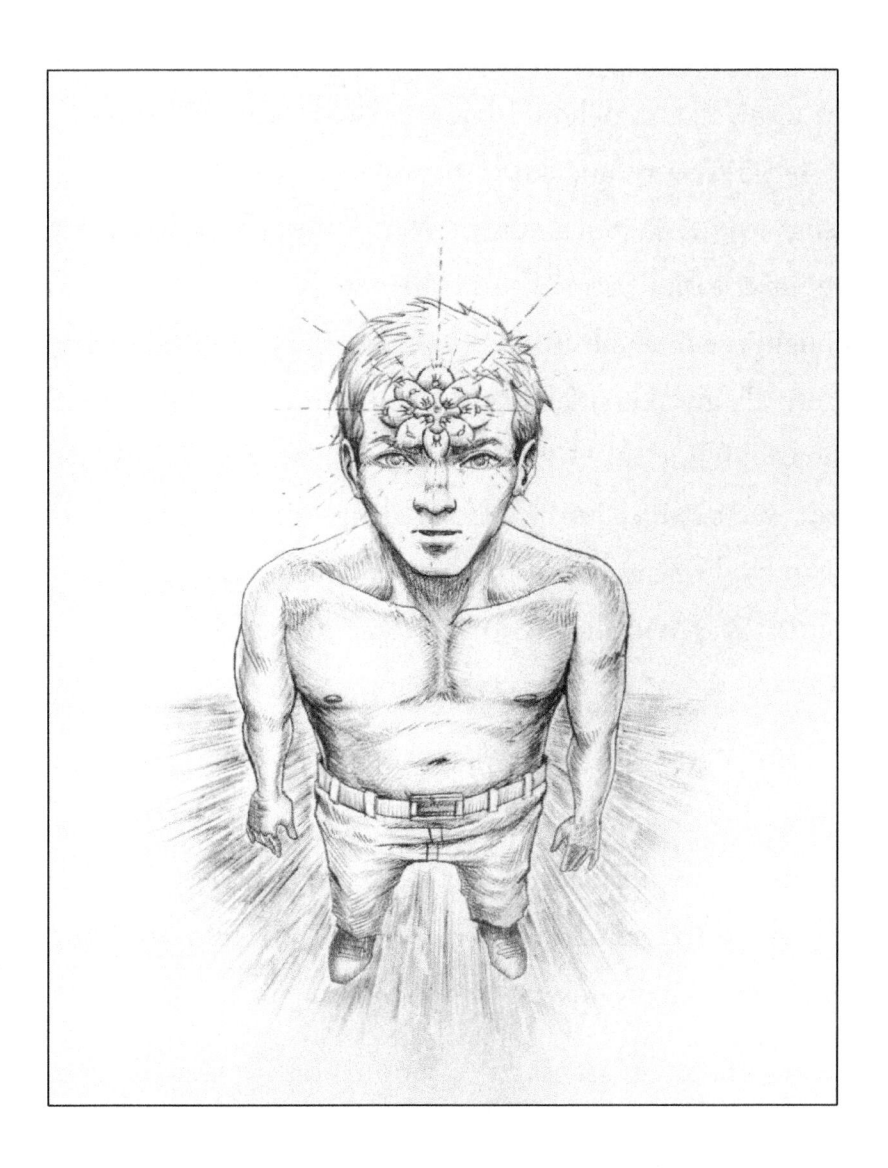

The Cactus of Sanity

I don't remember exactly from whom and when I heard the term "Third Eye" for the first time. But I do remember the feeling of being quite intrigued by the notion. It didn't sound to me crazy at all. I remember a sort of familiarity with this term, like somehow I knew what it meant. This passion for self-discovery and knowing what is possible for human beings led me to join a Fourth Way philosophical system that promised to lead a man to his highest potential, but instead brought me to a cult led by a Goddess trapped in man's body where all my potential was used in hard, slave-like physical labor, building an Ark for humanity, which, according to him, was destined to be destroyed by nuclear war. I shared this period of my life in my first book. That being said, the Fourth Way still did its job by opening me up to esoteric ideas and set me on the path of self-discovery.

I tried to find every description of the Third Eye in literature, but a description is never the thing it describes. Being disillusioned with theories and ineffective practices, I decided to seek a direct spiritual experience, which intuitively I knew would give me the answers I was searching for.

The unbroken Huachuma tradition of Peru that has been practiced for thousands of years confirmed that my search was not in vain. My very first Huachuma ceremony in the

Peruvian Amazon, in December 2005, showed me how much more there is to the notion of Third Eye and spirituality in general, taking me above words and concepts. During the first Huachuma ceremony I already knew that this would be my spiritual path in life. I finally found that which I was looking for.

The Third Eye is described as the mind's eye, the inner eye or an invisible eye, located in the middle of the forehead and is a responsible perception beyond ordinary sight. Hindus also place a "tilaka" between the eyebrows to represent it, which is also seen on depictions of Shiva. Buddhists regard the Third Eye as the "eye of consciousness," representing the vantage point from which enlightenment is achieved. I can confirm this is exactly where you feel it on Huachuma medicine. You can see it inside your head like an organ or a brain muscle of some sort and feel it like a portal, through which an intensified consciousness is perceived as a very bright, warm and ecstatic sensation.

The first time I experienced this was traveling in the Andes with Don Howard Lawler, my first shamanic teacher, while visiting the crystal-blue waters of Llanganuco Lake in Cordillera Blanca, a high-altitude lake that is also called the "mirror of the sky" for its pure blue water. Apart from being absolutely amazed by the experience, I entertained a troubling thought that said, "What if this never ends? What if I can never be normal again?" I remember sitting on the ground there and seeing my mind, helpless like a little child. Being the light myself, I saw my mind with compassion and understanding. "Everything is fine." Either I heard a voice coming from somewhere, or what I've heard was another thought in my head, but regardless of what it was and who said it, it felt good and relaxing. When I opened my eyes, I kept staring at the mountain's snowy peak, which was right in front of me. Its mystical beauty was beyond all description.

Don Howard was near me, looking at the same mountains. "There is God", he said quietly but firmly. His words resonated with me. This was the moment when the atheist in me died. I felt it. We talked for a while, and then he left me to myself. I put on music from the band Dead Can Dance, something I loved listening to, sat on the ground and just kept looking at the snowy mountains in front of me. Tears were coming down my face, tears of happiness, tears of knowing. The God I felt was not a figure in the sky. I've been in the sky many times, flying all over the world. I never saw anyone there. It was a Divine presence that I could feel in the lake, in the mountains, in its blindingly bright snow and in myself. It was solemn and sacred.

This was my first journey to Peru. I was at a crossroads in my life. I had left the Fellowship of Friends cult just a week prior to my travel, and my marriage to my first wife had ended for the same reason. I felt free, but it was painful at the same time. The world I knew was no longer, and the new world had yet to come. I saw it as a necessary payment that I had to make to find truth in my life.

Looking at it from the lake, I felt at peace. I recalled a passage from *In Search of the Miraculous* by Peter Ouspenksy, who helped G.I. Gurfjieff popularize the Fourth Way system in Russia. One of its premises was Gurdjieff's idea that the Law of Accidents governed people's lives from birth to death. Life just happens to people, no one is actually living it at will — an unconscious living that made us subject to external circumstances without having a say in our own fate. Life was also happening to me and many attempts to make a change had only shown how difficult it was to change anything. I was tired of being a victim of circumstances and my own stupidity that led me to all kinds of trouble. But things looked differently from the lake at 12,632 feet above sea level. Everything was clear, everything felt right. All that has

The Cactus of Sanity

happened to me has also formed my character. There I had a strong feeling that following my conscience was the right thing to do all along. I knew that life would be different from that point onward if I made a choice. So simple and so profound. Choosing the life I wanted to live was the only thing required. It felt like a simple truth, but it felt like a secret as well.

Why are we told that on the spiritual path we must dedicate our lives to a guru or a teaching, when in fact, all that is needed is a direct spiritual experience to figure things out for yourself? A lifelong dedication as a disciple might yield no results. How wasteful indeed. I now gratefully received outside help, which Gurdjieff said was needed, from the Huachuma cactus. It felt so real and liberating.

To call it all a Third Eye experience would be to diminish it, although technically speaking, the term would certainly apply. It can be called Oneness, Unity, Awakening, Enlightenment, Samadhi, Kundalini, a state of total equilibrium, the state of Pure Insight, or any other name different spiritual traditions have given to the same phenomenon of dissolution of the ego into the wholeness of Being. William Shakespeare's phrase, "A rose by any other name would smell as sweet," came to mind — just different names describing the same state of consciousness. You can call it what you like, but the experience of it remains what it is. The gates to higher consciousness are open, but you have to know what you are looking for in order to find it.

I can assure you that the Third Eye concept is not a metaphor. It can be argued that it is related to the activation or over-stimulation of the pineal gland, which René Descartes called a seat of the soul. The science behind it is unclear. But the spiritual sight beyond the physical is real, and it is available to be experienced with Huachuma. It could be that Huachuma delivers the sunlight to the gland, in a way that otherwise cannot happen. We cannot look directly at the sun without damaging our eyes, and we do not absorb sunlight sufficiently through the skull in order to produce mystical experiences. But this is speculation about a lesser riddle than the experience itself. Huachuma has an obvious direct impact on actual physical sight. I've hosted two people who suffered from nearsightedness, a condition that makes distant objects appear blurred. In both cases, at different times and locations, they reported a dramatic increase in their sight. One of them could spot an eagle far away in the clouds when, in fact, she could not see a person clearly just a few meters away. The other woman could distinguish and count trees in the forest, when in her normal condition the forest was blurry, like an abstract painting. There is a definite connection between Huachuma and visual perception.

I will tell one story to appropriately end this chapter. Many years ago, I was making different brews, lighter for people who had no experience and stronger for people with previous experiences with psychedelics and sacred plants. One day, I brewed a medicine in a special way, following my intuition. As usual, each new medicine I was making, I was trying it first on myself to see how strong it was before serving it to people. When I took it and went out to Nature, the world started to melt. By the river, I found a spot to lie down, since the best thoughts and deepest feelings come when I lie on the ground. I felt like I was going to fall through the Earth and appear somewhere in Australia. It was an effort to remain on the surface. My body felt as though it was made out of air. At one point I thought that holding onto a tree would be a good idea, to prevent me from flying away like a kite.

I was alarmed at first, but then I managed to keep calm and just go with it. When I reached for a bottle of water and looked at my hand, I saw through it like x-ray vision. It was transparent. If I had been able to write at this moment, I could have written a dissertation on human anatomy with one breath. Then, I looked at the tree. I could see through it as well. By the time I made an attempt to look through the mountain, I was already feeling on the edge of my capacity to cope with the experience. I felt like I was melting away, becoming one with the whole. I felt like I was everywhere and always at once, outside space and time. I was struggling to keep myself together from disappearing into the rays of Creation. It was perhaps the most astonishing and yet the most difficult place I've visited so far, for it was unbearable for the mind and the nervous system to handle. It comes with a tremendous amount of mind-shattering fear and deep purging. It's a nuclear strike on one's ego that only needs to be experienced once in a lifetime.

Huachuma is a visionary cactus that has as many dimensions as it has many ribs. My own brew gave me such a shattering experience in order to show me what it can do and how far it can take me. I called it an "air medicine" because of its air-like quality of being weightless and transparent. I never experienced anything like that with my Huachuma teachers, whose medicine was good and very potent. This experience keeps me humble as I continue working with Huachuma. I know its power. Upon "landing" from this cosmic voyage, I realized that you don't need to be overwhelmed in order to produce healing and mystical experience. Good lesson indeed.

To finalize this line of thought, I will only touch on the importance of the body that is neglected in some spiritual traditions. While some people entertain the idea of out of body experiences, I focus my work on the "in body" experience. The felt presence of your body grounded in Nature makes the experience what it is. An awakening without that strong bond with your body most likely only happens in your head. Gurdjieff was absolutely correct when he said, "It is only by grounding our awareness in the living sensation of our bodies that the 'I Am,' our real presence, can awaken."

CHAPTER 14

HUACHUMA, THE HOUSE BUILT ON THE ROCK

For a reader who read my previous books, my religious stance is clear. I won't go into it here, since an effort to write it down has already been made. Yet still, for the new reader, I think it is fair to boil it down. I am not a religious person in a general sense. I do not believe in God in the common religious sense. I do not affiliate with any religious organization. I hold my own beliefs, which are spiritual in essence, but not religious. This being said, I think we can learn from any religion if we practice discernment and know how to separate seed from chaff.

Personally, I'm looking for things that make sense and resonate with me. For example, here is a quote from the Bible that speaks about the importance of having a solid foundation for your faith:

"Everyone then who hears these words of mine and does them will be like a wise man who built his house on the rock. And the rain fell, and the floods came, and the winds blew and beat on that house, but it did not fall, because it had been founded on the rock. (Matthew 7:24-25)

The Cactus of Sanity

This is a self-evident truth, for it is true both in material and spiritual worlds. Building a spiritual house on the sand means betting on illusion. Building on stone means growing from roots firmly established in the earth. Huachuma is the holy water that allows your roots to grow deep into the Divine Ground. Huachuma solidifies your presence, your connection with yourself and Nature. It makes you see all aspects of human nature. Awakening has dual Nature. It makes you see the light and darkness and gives you the power to decide what gets into your mind. It makes your spirit poisonous to the fear-virus. It makes you very bitter, distasteful and even repulsive to the Beast. You starve it if it comes to you.

Huachuma is the narrow gate spoken of in the Bible: "Enter by the narrow gate. For the gate is wide and the way is easy that leads to destruction, and those who enter by it are many. For the gate is narrow and the way is hard that leads to life, and those who find it are few." (Matthew 7:13-14) The gate is narrow because it only has the space for your heart to enter.

When I began writing my first book, I had a dilemma. On one hand I wanted to share with everyone that incredible healing power of Huachuma and other plant teachers in order to help people heal and break the shackles of mental slavery. On the other, I was worried that the medicine work can get corrupted and distorted in the wrong hands, thus losing its power to heal and guide. Over the years I've heard about and met people who come to Peru, spend a very short time around the medicine, and got the impression that they can now build Ayahuasca Churches and Huachuma Temples and serve medicine to people just because they can play a guitar. I must warn against such false pretenses and inflated egos. It takes years of dedication, training and practice before a person is ready to serve medicine to others. Music is not an essential part of it. In fact, I don't employ music at all. Nature is my orchestra, my symphony is silence. I'm here to help you hear the beating of your heart.

CHAPTER 15

HUACHUMA AND THE MEANING OF LIFE

A search for meaning in life is a link that connects people throughout human history. Many of them have left their findings in writings, art and music. There are many others who were just as consumed by it but were not able to express themselves. A search for meaning seems to be a human need that, for some people, remains unexpressed. For whatever reason, my search for meaning began very early in life. I was five years old when I was already asking my parents where I was before I was born and where I will be after I die. Of course, my parents couldn't answer me. Reading many books written by spiritual teachers was helpful to a point. They only confirmed that my search was not something crazy, or out of line, but is a human thread. Yet still, I have not found specific and satisfactory answers. What I did realize by reading is that no one actually has answers for me. This is not to say that they didn't have any, but their findings were theirs to keep. I began to think that the meaning of life is a personal endeavor that must be found for oneself. It is not out there, like an object one can reach or like a planet one can see. It is more like a falling star that one glimpses briefly in the night sky, but when one tells others who are with him to look it up, they can only see darkness. Just as seeing the falling star is a personal experience, so is the search for meaning.

I never was ill. I had a spiritual problem I wanted to solve. The world was ill. Materialistic society was ill, and the existential void that it derives from was the spiritual sickness I saw many people suffer from. I found a way to satisfy my spiritual search, and I now help others to find theirs. But my findings are mine. And just as no one else can live your life, no one else can give your life meaning. You can spend a lifetime following a guru and sweeping an ashram just to realize that the truth of your guru, if he or she has it, was theirs and was only good as long as it helped you find your own. In the end, this effort did not resolve an inner conflict that was never a neurosis, but a state of being in which a living soul was looking for its own expression in life. Truth, just like meaning, is the personal experience of reality, not a static dogma. From this perspective, following a guru or a teaching is pointlessness, unless their aim is to help you find our own. It was painful to be a spiritual seeker constantly asking the same questions over and over again. A sweet sadness, a burning feeling and a deep longing were my only answers. A strong desire to leave a meaningful life with clarity, depth, magic and love has kept me going and looking.

The Cactus of Sanity

This desire to have a meaningful life has led to its fulfilment. It was a bumpy road but it led me to my destination. I never doubted its direction. Today I understand that, in fact, I trusted my fate. Deep down in my heart I knew I would find my way. Now I find meaning in love and in work. My family and my work with sacred Huachuma medicine is what I live for, is what I love, is what I want.

My books and my films are only the expression of this inner satisfaction and self-contentment. It is a way to express gratitude. Huachuma has shown me that my life experiences were my treasure, my assets and my friends. I had the choice to either bury them in the archives of memory and let them be wasted, or accept them and make them serve a purpose. It helped me see value in my past, something that I hadn't seen before.

The Third Eye experience that you read in a book or hear about from spiritual teachers is real but it is still on the level of the psyche. Huachuma takes you where your third eye becomes the eye of the Universe, through which you can see with your mind. Huachuma is an introspective medicine that allows you to look deep into yourself. It helps you put things in perspective and see your life from a necessary distance, thus allow you to see a bigger picture. I see existence as the meaning of life as much as life is the meaning of existence. What is the point of being alive without being conscious of it? Being conscious of your life is what gives it meaning. I love my life. It is meaningful to me. I would be happy to relive it over and over again without asking for anything to change.

Huachuma is able to make you see the significance of both sacred and trivial things. When you dissolve in an infinite light where there is no longer anything but Oneness, you realize that even this state is meaningless without love. Love is the fifth element that makes the other four relevant and valuable. Love is the reason for all that exists. Nothing is trivial when you are

The Cactus of Sanity

fully conscious. Everything has its place and its meaning. For example, we just take a sunrise for granted, when, in fact, there is so much meaning in it. Living in the West, I always considered myself a night person. I went to sleep very late or in fact, very early in the morning, hiding from a sunrise that at that time signified another day of a routine and a struggle. This changed after I moved to Peru. Often I get impatient during the night in the anticipation of the sunrise, where there is so much energy. Today, I value each day. Each new sunrise is another chance to live another day with love.

Huachuma gently shows that your life matters and it has a meaning. It shows you that there is more to you than a consumer, a taxpayer, a human resource, a believer and a cultural product. It reminds you that you are a product of love and love is what you need to pursue in order to stay in the zone, in the state of heightened awareness, focus and inspiration. Huachuma is the antidote to apathy. It wakes you up to your life and makes you witness the Divine existence of which you are a part. It makes you feel the wind that blows freedom in your face. That freedom is you. That freedom is love. It makes you realize that all of your previous struggle in life was needed to form your character and make you feel worthy of your past as your past becomes worthy of you. By helping you to peel off the layers of falsehood and pretense, it brings you to your genuine, authentic self. From this new perspective, life looks different. You might realize that your inner struggle, that sweet sorrow with which you lived your daily life, was your medicine all along, your compass that has finally led you to yourself.

It was actually on LSD when I saw my future. Got to give credit where credit is due. Having taken a tab of acid in my home in Sacramento, California, I realized that my destiny was in Peru. I strongly felt that I had to move there and follow the Huachuma path. To be honest, I got a bit nervous. I had to

The Cactus of Sanity

leave the United States, where I had lived for 8 years and got used to a certain level of comfort. Starting all over again in a new culture and learning a new language felt like a challenge. I immediately wrote an email to Don Howard, with whom I had already spent time in Peru working with plant medicine on numerous occasions, and told him that I knew my destiny, but I don't know if I am ready for it. His prompt answer helped me calm down.

That night I spent outside, sitting by the Huachuma cacti growing in my backyard, listening to crickets. The decision to move to Peru was made that night, even though it took some time to manifest. I realized that I answer to no one but myself, and following my heart was my responsibility. That was my meaning to be fulfilled. My hope to find my path had carried me to this point, now it was time for action.

So, what is the right way to live? I can only give a general rule, which I came up with from personal struggle. The only right answer to me is living your life the way it feels right to you. The only path in life worth taking is the one that has heart. When you are shaken out of your cultural and religious programming, you will find it for yourself. It is the same with meaning. I now think that this is the hidden truth that I always have felt has existed — truth that was not to be found in pentagrams and ancient texts. I have looked there too.

How can anyone tell you what the meaning of your life is? If you ask a painter what is the best color to use in paintings, he or she would answer that this would depend on the content of the painting, on the season and the time of the day that an artist is trying to convey. Days would be painted with brighter colors than nights, and an expression of happiness would require different shading than sadness. All colors, they would say, serve their purpose and are best when used accordingly. The same, I would say, is true when we paint the picture of our lives. Sometimes the context requires patience and acceptance, other times action. The right move is different to different people at different times. When we are waiting for life to give us a chance, patience is a virtue that prevents us from acting prematurely and deviating from our path. But when the chance is given, waiting has to be replaced with action. The windows of opportunities are not static. They move with time. They are more like a window of a train that, after a short time at the station, starts moving faster and faster until you realize that you have missed it.

What is the meaning of life? Why do I live? Why do I wake up every morning? What is it that I have to do? What are the rules?

The Cactus of Sanity

Who are the players? How much time is given to play the game of life? These are a few of the questions I was pondering all along, among others. Pondering these questions once again on Huachuma high up in the mountains of Peru, seeking answers among the stunningly beautiful snow peaks, for the first time I felt that my inner monologues had been heard by the spirit:

What was the meaning of my life? I realized that this kind of question can only be answered on a personal level, and a specific answer can only be given to a specific question.

Why do I live? Because you were given a chance.

Why do I wake up every morning? To learn and love.

What do I have to do? Fulfil your meaning.

What are the rules? You make your own.

Who are the players? Just time.

How much time do I have? I heard only silence in response.

I opened my eyes, thinking, what kind of a dream did I just have? Did I actually talk to someone, or was it all in my head? A gentle wind gusted nearby. It felt like someone's presence. The ancient ruins of the Eagle's Nest had been abandoned over a thousand years ago, and it was just me out there.

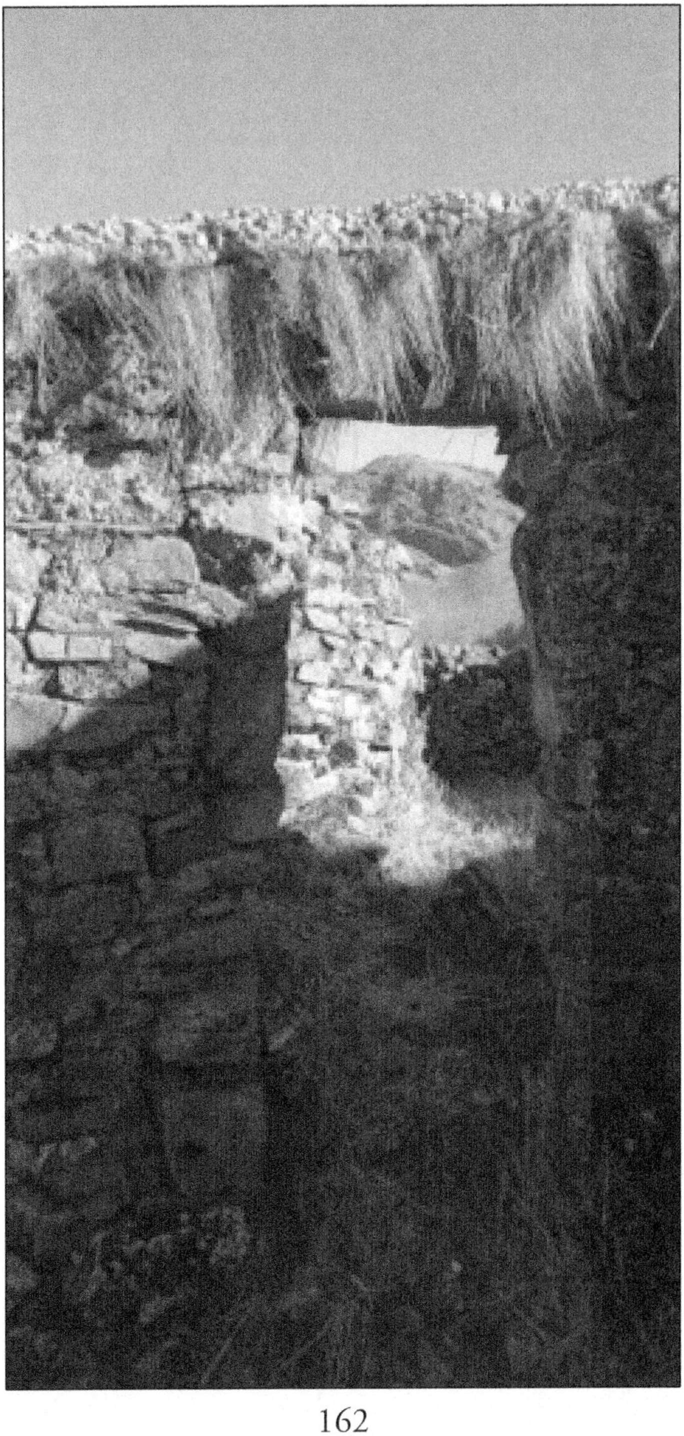

PART III

DIAGNOSING THE MODERN WORLD

CHAPTER 16

CONSCIOUSNESS IN EXILE: A SHAMANIC PERSPECTIVE

Humanity has reached a point in history where major decisions have to be made. As we approach an existential crisis as a species, we must rethink and re-evaluate our way of life, and the outcome of this deeply introspective process will determine our future. Just as every individual goes through personal crises during the growth process, we are collectively at such a crisis point now. Adolescent, irresponsible and silly, we seem to think we understand the world and know better than those who came before us, but we have no apparent guardian to guide us on our path, like a teenager can rely on his parents. We are told that we have such guidance in religious leaders, gurus, babas, self-proclaimed prophets and the luminaries of science, but, from personal experience and a lifelong spiritual search, I have come to the conclusion that nobody really knows, and none of these self-declared mentors possess a cure for personal and collective madness. Their methods, therapies and ideas are only mildly effective in helping with minor issues.

The Cactus of Sanity

This is what psychology is all about. When it comes to serious problems such as the need for purpose and meaning — Why live or not, and if yes, then how? — mainstream psychology, religion and spirituality can only hook you up to their life-support machines via soothing words or pharmaceuticals. You will live, with the aid of these brittle crutches, but your life will have little taste and color. This is, in fact, the message I seek to deliver, the message I hear in my heart: the simple, clear voice of Mother Earth. This purely intuitive yet rational communication would most likely fit psychiatry's description of schizophrenia, but I assure you that it would not be difficult for me to confront anyone from the field and convince them otherwise.

There is nothing crazy about loving and communing with the heart, blood and lungs of the planet. That which makes the planet live is currently sick, perhaps even dying. There is nothing insane about feeling a bond with Nature and finding healing peace in it. There is nothing strange about enjoying the sound of birds, the rivers, the feel of sunshine and warm wind. There is nothing weird about feeling a spiritual bond with animals and plants we share this planet with. And there is nothing wrong about seeking physical, emotional, mental and spiritual healing by using sacred plants. Unfortunately, these great teachers are seized and suppressed by those who do not have our best interests at heart. These are the people who have assumed the divine right to command others. Of course, their sense of superiority is utterly false and the product of a continuum of illusions: digits on the screen, media attention, fancy banquets and red carpets. But these only signify material wealth, which translates into social influence. If, however, such "masters" were to appear in front of a jury, judged on a moral standard, perhaps most of them would be found guilty.

None of my friends would support a law to send people to kill others and get killed themselves. None of my friends would support corporate fascism run rampant, destroying our environment and the lives of our children to make more money. None of my friends would bail out banks while letting working families have their lives ruined. None of my friends would support a lifestyle by which some die from obesity while others starve to death. None of my friends would criminalize safe and effective plant medicines while making experimental and dangerous pharmaceutical drugs legal. But none of my friends are bankers, corporate heads and politicians. Thus, like me, they are forced to live under the iron fist of unjust law.

The Cactus of Sanity

Unfortunately, this is the true history of our world. Perhaps it was different before the creation of money. People fished and hunted to get fed and no one was in control of their lives. Their natural needs motivated them. This was also before the preacher existed. No one was stupid enough to endanger their lives hunting a bear just to give a portion of it to someone who would tell him about the glory of a mysterious afterlife about which the preacher could truly know nothing. No one would give a piece of meat in exchange for shallow words. People were pragmatic because life demanded them to be so. No one would leave their family in a cave to follow a weirdo who claims that he is the reincarnated Christ, or others who say that enlightenment is just a lifetime ahead.

So why today, being evolved in so many ways, do we retain childish, illogical, absurd notions and idiotic beliefs when it comes to the core of our lives: our freedom? Why, today, do we stand around like drunk people, silently and passively observing our own execution?

Why, today, are we fed pharmaceuticals while an abundance of consciousness-expanding, healing plants are known and available? These plants are accessible and very effective. By rejecting this hand given to us by Nature, we reject the opportunity to heal, understand ourselves and the world. If our world is made of cognition, then consciousness is the fuel we need most. And if sacred plants can easily seed the fields of our minds and grow consciousness, then this is where we must direct our resources.

Can you imagine the impact on human life if the purchase of just one fighter jet F-35 was cut so that $135 million could be directed toward consciousness research? Can you imagine the impact on our health if the purchase of just one nuclear submarine was canceled and its $1.7 billion were given to independent researchers in search of a cure for cancer? Can you fathom the results on our education if the purchase of one aircraft carrier was shelved and $13 billion were given to a group of the brightest individuals and educators of our time to work together and create a better curriculum for our kids? Or if a mere fraction of it could be given to the brightest engineers to fashion the technology we need to power the Earth with alternative, clean sources of energy? Can you imagine our world without hunger and poverty? All it takes is the cancellation of a few wars! It seems to me that the evolutionists have missed the point. Instead of arguing over the origin of man and searching for the missing link between

The Cactus of Sanity

monkeys and humans, they should be searching for the missing links between humans.

I see an urgent need for a collective effort to fund independent consciousness research via psychedelics, attracting the best hearts and minds we have. We need to take our world back and let human potential be realized in a constructive way. Disempowered by the lack of a direct spiritual experience, we are floating away from the treasure island that is our planet Earth. We are willing to invest so much in destructive technologies, but we ignore the technology we already have to explore our consciousness: sacred plants. Psychedelic experience brings people together and lets them see their commonalities as greater than their differences. We even have professional technicians to operate the equipment. All we need is a change in law, which holds everything back. In fact, it holds back the survival and evolution of our species, which makes psychedelic prohibition a crime against humanity.

Psychedelics can open many doors and their greatest gift, at this vital moment, is the realization that our world is worth saving. Our industrialized culture has many tanks: We have fuel tanks, water tanks, military tanks and even "think-tanks," but we don't have a significant "psychedelic tank" that a sane world could lawfully assemble to help us grasp higher consciousness. Such a group of individuals working together, not needing to compete individually just to put food on their plates, would gather momentum to heighten consciousness, to develop a social sanity out of which better ideas would emerge. However, with the pressure of modern life, restrained by time, money and freedom, enormous human potential is being lost. It's great to have a sensory deprivation tank where you go to relax somewhere in the city. But we need a psychedelic tank just as much, to roll over the insanity and delusion which seems to rise with every single day. What kind of a society have we created, where people's connection with one another is through misery and pain? It feels hopeless if it goes unchanged, like there is no way out of the vicious circle.

Spiritually deprived and unhappy, you are forced through daily drudgery. Have you ever used a subway in New York or London? This is how millions of people start and end each day: in a dark, cold, noisy, unfriendly environment, full of people who, just like you, hate to be there. They are unwitting companions on your life journey. Did you ever ask yourself why you live in the city? Did it ever occur to you that a toxic city life may be the root cause for depression and anxiety? Artificial modern culture exacerbates the problem. Out of desperation and loneliness people fall into all kinds of addictions, join bizarre cults and believe in strange, circular ideas, all just to escape their misery. Others end their lives.

Intuitively, we feel the need to restore the inner and outer order. But this task is impossible without the help of our immeasurably intelligent plant teachers, which have withstood the test of millions of years of evolution and are available to heal the self-hating, neurotic egos that have been programmed into us. We are told by spiritual leaders that we don't need psychedelic plants, that it's just enough to cross our legs and focus our attention on our nose and breathing. This might work in a city as a way to come back to your center after a busy day in work. But, to make changes in your life, it takes more than leg crossing. These are slow-acting technologies and we have run out of time to rely upon them. We are, and have been for millennia, gravitating towards Nature and shamanic ecstasy. A symbiosis between us and the natural world is not a fantasy but a fundamental law of Nature and a force as certain as gravity. And just as particles are pulled together by the force of gravity, we are pulled together by the innate desire to connect.

What kind of a world are we living in today when a Law of Nature is illegal to practice? Religion is a child of psychedelic experiences that has denounced his parent. Spiritual leaders fail us, like our philosophers and political leaders. They are all pursuing their own agenda, while caring less for the rest of us. Humanity is the prodigal son that must return home. Wretched, lost, fallen into poverty and despair, it crawls back to Nature for help. This is what I see in Rembrandt's classic painting, "The Return of the Prodigal Son." Besides the clear message of forgiveness and mercy, masterfully represented by the Dutch artist, I see humanity represented by the Prodigal Son, and Mother Nature in the figure of the father. This painting is an archetype for spiritual awakening, an insight that takes it out of religious context. It is time to embrace life and reclaim our hearts and minds.

The plants are real and their dimensions are accessible for us. Clear thinking leads to evolution, confusion leads to extinction, and that is the truth. We don't have scarcity of resources and plants. We only lack guidance and a legal climate in which we can comfortably explore consciousness. In the absence of psychedelics, our egos grow like cancer, eventually consuming the host. We think we are becoming Gods by being able to split the atom and slice genes, a dangerous technology without humility and spiritual understanding. But in fact, we may be becoming arrogant morons who are on the brink of destroying everything that has been created on Earth by humanity and the Universe. There is another way to move forward.

While genetic science is busy editing genes, sacred medicine can help you edit your reality and become the author of your own life. This is the true essence of ancient alchemy, which never was about turning lead into gold but rather transforming your fear into love and transcending the mechanical, mindless aspects of human existence. This inner transformation is what we are after, the same kind that the ancient alchemists were striving for — the inner gold, not a shiny metal found in the ground. Just like the ancient alchemists, we want to escape determinism and become the masters of our own lives.

CHAPTER 17

MILITARIZED PSYCHIATRY VS. PLANT MEDICINE

"A spoon of cactus juice a day keeps the doctor away."

— The Author

A new development in the psychiatric field deserves attention, but not because it is promising and hopeful. A recent article[5] published by the University of North Carolina makes a few important points. First is the official admission that current psychiatric drugs have serious side effects.

"Rapidly acting drugs to treat depression, anxiety, or substance abuse without side effects do not exist. Researchers led by Bryan L. Roth, MD, PhD, the Michael Hooker Distinguished Professor of Pharmacology at the UNC School of Medicine, are trying to change that. With a four-year, $27-million cooperative agreement from the Defense Advanced Research Project Agency (DARPA), Roth and colleagues will use new structural biology and computational approaches to create new medicines that work rapidly and effectively without serious side effects." Roth later adds,

The Cactus of Sanity

"Rapidly acting drugs with antidepressant, anti-anxiety, and anti-addictive potential devoid of disabling side effects do not exist, not even as experimental compounds for use in animals. Creating such compounds would change the way we treat millions of people around the world suffering from these serious and life-threatening conditions."

For many years, people in the field of alternative medicine have been vocal on the subject. Seeing people actually cure severe depression after only a few weeks of engagement with different plant medicines leaves them no choice but to share the good news with other fellow human beings and help them stop their mental suffering. Helping one another is a human thread — unless, of course, big money gets involved and changes the focus. Psychiatry has nearly lost its meaning since its merger with Big Pharma, which has basically turned a psychiatrist into a legal drug dealer. Busy prescribing, they have little time to provide actual therapy. But the prescribed medications, of course, are only good for short term treatment that simply masks the symptoms and gets you back to work. In fact, they should be labeled productivity boosters rather than psychiatric medicines.

No psychiatric drugs are capable of curing depression, simply because depression is a symptom of a wounded soul that will continue to suffer, regardless of the amount of drugs pumped into a body. Drugs disrupt the healthy signals coming from the depth of our psyches, telling us that something is wrong and needs attention. Instead of looking inwards and trying to figure out what needs healing, one is prescribed medications that block this signal. But the problem still persists, even when one is drugged and numb to it. In fact, it will worsen over time, since all mental health disorders have the potential for negative effects occur if left untreated.

According to Lancet[6], the most prestigious medical journal in the world, "depression is a major public health problem; it is a leading contributor to the global burden of disease, affecting hundreds of millions of people worldwide, and costing the USA alone more than US$200 billion each year." People who suffer through chronic distress associated with mental health disorders can experience chemical changes in their organs, which can lead to physical problems. It also affects personal relationships with family and friends, which can lead to a number of issues, such as divorce, losing friends and isolation. Fatigue and apathy will negatively affect work and daily living. This may result in substance abuse as a form of escape from reality. Alcoholism, legal and illegal drug abuse are likely to follow. Attempted suicide is what awaits many at the end of this road.

Just think of a person who constantly suffers from headache. Instead of seeing a doctor, he might only take pain killers to help and keep doing it until his brain blew up from hypertension, which he was suffering from without knowing it. The hypertension was the cause of his headache and should have been diagnosed and addressed directly. Masking the symptoms with pain killers was a short-term solution that led to his premature death.

Another analogy can be drawn from your car. Your engine requires oil to function. The dashboard oil light comes on when your engine suffers a drop in oil pressure. Without enough oil pressure, the engine can't lubricate itself and can stop abruptly, causing severe engine damage and an accident. Will turning off the dashboard light fix the problem of low oil pressure? Of course, not. The problem will persist until fixed or the engine breaks. Antidepressants, too, just mask symptoms while allowing the inner crisis to continue. Pharmacology is an ancient science, but pharmacology without therapy is just drugging the symptoms into oblivion, which seems to be the best modern psychiatry and pharmacology can offer. From an economic perspective, it is an excellent business model -- it creates customers for life. But the economy should take a back seat when it comes to health, at least in a sane and moral society.

While Dr. Roth is correct in regard to pharmaceuticals, the whole range of natural medicine is available to treat and cure depression, anxiety, and addictions without side effects. Plant medicine does not have side effects. It may sound too good to be true to a Westerner who has never heard of plant medicine shamanism. However, those who have used plant medicines for healing can confirm it.

Here is a warning that comes on the insert of Prozac[7], an antidepressant that is often prescribed to treat depression:

WARNING: SUICIDALITY AND ANTIDEPRESSANT DRUGS

Antidepressants increased the risk compared to placebo of suicidal thinking and behavior (suicidality) in children, adolescents, and young adults in short-term studies of Major Depressive Disorder (MDD) and other psychiatric disorders. Anyone considering the use of PROZAC or any other antidepressant in a child, adolescent, or young adult must balance this risk with the clinical need. Short-term studies did not show an increase in the risk of suicidality with antidepressants compared to placebo in adults beyond age 24; there was a reduction in risk with antidepressants compared to placebo in adults aged 65 and older. Depression and certain other psychiatric disorders are themselves associated with increases in the risk of suicide. Patients of all ages who are started on antidepressant therapy should be monitored appropriately and observed closely for clinical worsening, suicidality, or unusual changes in behavior. Families and caregivers should be advised of the need for close observation and communication with the prescriber."

It further states, "There has been a long-standing concern, however, that antidepressants may have a role in inducing worsening of depression and the emergence of suicidality in certain patients during the early phases of treatment. Pooled analyses of short-term placebo-controlled trials of antidepressant drugs (SSRIs and others) showed that these drugs increase the risk of suicidal thinking and behavior (suicidality) in children, adolescents, and young adults (ages 18-24) with Major Depressive Disorder and other psychiatric disorders."

So, you take a drug that is supposed to help you cope with your depression only to find out that the risk of suicide has been now increased, and you should be closely monitored.

Nevertheless, this drug is FDA approved for safety and human consumption. How safe is it if it increases the risk of your own death? I assume that logic is a principle that should be applied in medicine. A fallacy such this simply weakens the argument for pharmaceuticals.

As the fact of serious side effects of antidepressants has been established, we now need to look at the proposed solution to the problem. DARPA has funded the development of better medication, raising more concerns. In an article titled, "Structure-Guided Drug Design Could Yield Fast-Acting Remedies for Complex Neuropsychiatric Conditions,[8]" DARPA presents a new program called Focused Pharma, which "will pursue new drugs that work quickly and deliver lasting remedies for conditions such as chronic depression and post-traumatic stress." In it, DARPA both confirms the undesirable side effects of antidepressants and admits that patients relapse once they stop taking them, creating addiction. They are habit-forming drugs that are prescribed for life. A relapse is inevitable as soon as the person stops taking them:

"At present, psychotherapy, psychopharmacology, and direct brain stimulation are the most effective means of treating the symptoms of neuropsychiatric conditions. While valuable, these approaches also have substantial drawbacks that make them less than ideal for treating a challenge on the scale of mental healthcare for the military community. Existing medications exhibit variable effectiveness from one individual to another, can lead to undesirable side effects, can take weeks to months to observe therapeutic benefits even when paired with counseling, and do nothing to prevent relapse once a patient stops taking them. In the case of psychotherapy and direct brain stimulation, finite availability of treatment makes it difficult to meet high demand over wide areas, and direct brain stimulation requires surgery."

The article further describes the mechanism of the new drugs:

"The goal of the Focused Pharma program is to develop novel compounds that directly affect specific neurotransmitter signaling processes that are often implicated in neurophysiological dysfunction, while overcoming limitations of current approaches. The envisioned drugs would selectively target and bind to specific neurotransmitter receptors, and activate only specific neural signaling pathways that may impact the conditions of interest."

Neurons communicate with one another via chemical and electronic means. One neuron sends a message to another neuron. Neurotransmitters are the chemical messengers released from neurons to "talk" to other neurons. Receptors, on the other hand, are the cells that "hear" the message. In other words, a new drug will filter and choose which neural signaling in a brain should be allowed by artificially disrupting the neurotransmitters' communication with the receptors. To return to my car analogy, imagine your brain is a car dashboard whose lights could be switched off at will. What happens if your oil light is switched off and you keep driving without oil? You destroy your engine.

Another important revelation can be found in DARPA's report. On one hand they admit the therapeutic value of psychedelic substances, and on the other, they dismiss it due to the "side effects" they call "hallucination."

"In creating Focused Pharma, DARPA examined evidence from privately funded human clinical studies demonstrating that certain Schedule 1 controlled drugs that engage serotonin receptors show promise of rapid and long-lasting therapeutic effect in treating neuropsychiatric conditions such as chronic alcohol dependence, post-traumatic stress, and treatment-resistant depression following only limited doses. However, because such drugs act on many neurotransmitter receptors and receptor subtypes in the brain without specificity and indiscriminately activate numerous signaling pathways, they produce significant side effects, including hallucination. These effects, coupled with their unpredictable consequences, render the drugs unusable in a military healthcare setting."

I thoroughly explore the subject of "hallucination" vs. visions, which are the language of plant medicines, in my previous book, *The Mescaline Confession: Breaking Through the Walls of Delusion*. Here, I would like to draw attention to what appears to me to be a discrepancy. All the studies that have been done on psilocybin were done predominantly with micro-dosing, which means the usage of a minimal effective dose that does not create "hallucination." Micro-dosing, or what I call a therapeutic dose, a dose that is low enough that is unlikely to produce a fully blown psychedelic effect but high enough to allow the cellular response to be felt and observed. I wouldn't be able to write this chapter if I took a full dose of Huachuma medicine. I would be sitting by the river now, merging with the Universe. But a micro-dose of Huachuma allows me to stay home and use my computer for writing.

A quite revealing and unbiased article published in *Lancet* titled, "Psilocybin with psychological support for treatment-resistant depression: an open-label feasibility study[9]" makes a number of important revelations. First it affirms the millennia-long use of psilocybin for healing: "Psilocybin is a naturally occurring plant alkaloid found in the Psilocybe genus of mushrooms. Psilocybe mushrooms have been used for millennia for healing purposes but were only discovered by modern science in the late 1950s." Its language omits the word "shamanism," the oldest spiritual healing practice in the world, which used different plant medicines for physical and mental healing. Nevertheless, it cites the historical fact that often gets ignored by academia and science.

The article further speaks of health benefits of plant medicines and confirms their safety: "Enhanced cognitive flexibility, associative learning, cortical neural plasticity, and antidepressant responses have been reported with 5-HT2A receptor agonism in animals, and increased and sustained improvements in wellbeing and optimism have been observed after psychedelic experiences in human beings. Findings from human imaging studies with psilocybin have supplemented these discoveries, showing changes in brain activity suggestive of antidepressant potential; for example, a range of effective antidepressant treatments have been found to normalize hyperactivity in the medial prefrontal cortex and we found reduced blood flow in this region with intravenous psilocybin. Moreover, data obtained from large-scale population studies have recently challenged the view that psychedelics negatively affect mental health, with one study's findings showing lower rates of psychological distress and suicidality among people who had used psychedelics within their lifetime than among those who used no psychedelics but an equivalent amount of other drugs. In modern trials, psychedelics have been found to reduce anxious, depressive, and obsessive-compulsive symptoms, as well as addictive behaviours, often for several months after just one or two exposures. Extensive historical and modern evidence now supports the view that, administered in a controlled environment with appropriate support, psychedelics have a favourable safety profile."

It goes on to relate the rapid reduction in depressive symptoms just after one psilocybin or Ayahuasca session, which lasted for weeks: "We also found one report documenting enduring decreases in depressive symptoms after a single dose of psilocybin in a randomised controlled trial of psilocybin-assisted psychotherapy for end-of-life anxiety, one report on an open-label trial showing rapid decreases in depressive symptoms that endured for up to 21 days after a single dose of ayahuasca, and two early reports or case studies on the effects of lysergic acid diethylamide on 'neurotic' and depressive symptoms describing 'improvements,' albeit without validated measures of symptom severity." This shows the effectiveness of plant medicine with only one session. This is also why at our retreat center, we recommend at least five to seven consecutive sessions during a two week period to facilitate deeper and lasting healing. During this time the plant medicine has a chance to recalibrate brain chemistry, which often results in permanent healing.

The *Lancet* study encourages "further research into the efficacy of psilocybin with psychological support for major depression. Larger-scale randomised controlled trials are warranted to better examine the potential of psilocybin as a treatment option for this highly prevalent, disabling, costly, and difficult-to-treat disorder. More broadly, the present study should help to catalyse the re-emergence of a promising research area in psychiatry."

I am not a psilocybin person, I am a mescaline guy. I don't have a dog in this fight. But fair is fair and credit must be given when credit is due. These, of course, are baby steps by science, but steps in the right direction nevertheless.

The Cactus of Sanity

Personally, for me, there is no debate on the subject. I know from experience the healing potential of Ayahuasca and, particularly, the Huachuma cactus, which has proven its efficacy to me way over a thousand times. For anyone who has taken a serious look at psychedelics, the notion of revolutionizing psychiatry by designing new drugs is no different than reinventing the wheel. The medicine wheel was created before humanity rose from its primitive state and perhaps was assisted by sacred plants on the way to its current condition. Reinventing the medicine wheel is not an attempt to revolutionize medicine, since the revolution has already happened in a prehistoric distant past. Most likely, it is about market shares and a desire to get deeper inside our minds. One way to look at why DARPA speaks unfavorably about psilocybin treatment of soldiers is that by taking psilocybin, a soldier might suddenly realize that being a soldier and being ready to die for a paycheck and make a living by killing is not the best way to spend his life.

The prospect that soldiers may quit as an "undesirable" effect of psilocybin treatment is perhaps the sole reason that DARPA rejects making it available for them. The same is true for civilians who, after a psychedelic experience, suddenly realize that they were not doing what they wanted in life. I've heard many stories about people who, after just one such experience, changed careers. This, of course, leads to personal healing, for a person cannot be happy if he hates the job to which he dedicates most of his time and energy. Psychedelics make you think for yourself, and that is the reason why they are heavily controlled by the powers that shouldn't be. To better understand this subject, I would highly recommend reading Aldous Huxley's 1931 dystopian novel, *Brave New World*. Written almost a century ago, it describes our modern drug-addled, brainwashed society in shocking detail. Huxley saw the future.

There is also another concern which might not be known even to the researchers. What are the long-term effects of these new drugs on your receptors? Will they still be active after the drugs' chemical targeting? If your receptors burn out, it will make you insensitive to plants. Psychedelic experience will be impossible for you in the future. In other words, it will make you psychoactively infertile. And just as sterilized people cannot procreate, you will not be able to produce psychedelic experiences when taking any substances or plants. On the contrary, we know that plant medicine does not fry receptors and does not have negative side effects. It is highly compatible with human physiology and psychology, and its testing time is measured by thousands of years of cultural experience. Approved for safety and effectiveness by either God or the force of evolution, whichever you prefer to believe, it is here to help us heal, reconnect and cherish life.

Another worrisome trend is coming from Silicon Valley. One would expect this field to be confined within digital walls. However, for reasons we can only guess, Silicon Valley is now moving into the field of health care, pharmacology and medicine. The merger of Big Tech with Big Pharma is described in the article "When two worlds collide — big pharma meets big tech."[10] It is not hard to imagine a future when your thoughts will be edited like genes, and your inner content gets deleted like politically incorrect Facebook posts that moderators deem to go against community standards.

I trust Mother Nature, who has withstood the test of time, more than digital technology for drug discovery. I choose to follow the intelligence of the Earth rather than algorithms and artificial minds. But if that wasn't enough to worry about, now there is DARPA's involvement in mental health care. Militarized psychiatry sounds an alarm for anyone who is aware of MK-Ultra, a top-secret CIA project in which the agency conducted hundreds of experiments on people to assess the potential use of LSD and other drugs for mind control, interrogation, information gathering and psychological torture. The program came to the public eye only in 1975 during congressional investigations into illegal CIA activities within the United States and abroad. Considering that this dark episode of the U.S. government lasted for 20 years and ruined countless minds by forcing LSD on people without their consent or knowledge, DARPA's involvement in mental health raises serious concerns. It's hard to trust a Terminator in white robe.

From talking to many people of different ages, genders and countries over the years who all have suffered from depression and were prescribed different antidepressants at different times, I saw a recurring pattern in their reports, among them, the feeling of partial living. It was as though a part of their brain was turned off by the prescribed medication so they could not think about their problems, and another part was turned on, so that they could go to work. Convinced by their doctors that this new feeling of being themselves was healthy and normal, they did not entertain the idea of seeking healing from plants. This half-living was the best pharmaceutical solution to a problem. But not being able to think about your problems does not fix your problems. The problems persist and worsen with time. Plant medicine takes you directly to your problem so you can see it, understand it and heal by making necessary changes in your life. Healing comes with understanding and clarity. The chemical part of it is automatic and needs no interference.

Mental health issues certainly require a lot of attention, and using plant medicine is certainly one right approach. However, and this must be said, treating sacred plants merely as natural antidepressants that are only useful to help with mental issues is like suggesting that a bazooka is only good for shooting birds. There is so much more to plant medicine than depression treatment, which is simply ignored by mainstream science. Science acts as though shamanic cultures have never existed, or if they did, their millennia-old, rich traditions and knowledge of healing plants have no value. Nothing is further from the truth. In fact, its value is hard to overstate.

In the light of current events and a growing competition for the human mind, it becomes urgent to resort to Nature that actually heals. It is time to reclaim one's mind from psycho-pharmaceutical dependency and give Nature a chance. We don't need new drugs. What we need is to return to Mother Nature. It works.

CHAPTER 18

THE ESSENCE OF HUACHUMA CACTUS

Anyone who has experienced a well-made Huachuma brew would testify that the essence of their experience is Love. And it truly is. Pure, unconditional, Divine love. This extraordinary but real experience is deeply healing on every level. It is simply self-evident, experiential truth. This medicine is a map for inner treasure, that very treasure that the mystics and the sages of antiquity knew about and some of whom possessed.

Living in the modern world is different, as illustrated in the film *The Matrix*. The modern Matrix appears wide open and promises total freedom. Yet it is a very constricted space for the soul, where spiritually mature people feel suffocated. In modern society there is simply no time or space for the Spirit. I know this for a fact. I came from there. And the fast-paced world is accelerating, driving its habitants deeper into disconnectedness and madness. For some, it is already a reality. Suppose you are already angry, frustrated and tired of waking up early on a cold, rainy day to drive to a job that you hate that is supervised by someone you don't like. It is already depressing as it is. Then, you get stuck in traffic,

The Cactus of Sanity

worrying that you will be late to the job that you hate doing. By the time you get to your workplace, you have already spent half of your daily energy, which melts under the pressure of negative emotions and fears, like snow under the sun. And your day just got started. To deal with mind fog and tiredness you drink many cups of coffee that stimulate you during the day by taxing your body at the end of it. Others use so-called "smart drugs," which in reality are not smart at all. It is just a marketing label used to sell them to you.

By the time you go home, you are barely the same person who left in the morning. Physically tired and emotionally drained, you come home like from a war zone, ready to numb yourself with alcohol and drugs. Spending the whole week in this way, you don't have enough time to recover over the weekend, when you drink more alcohol and do more drugs to escape reality. But of course, it doesn't work. Your escape is temporary and doesn't last. Your reality hits you in the face the next morning. Barely able to talk from a hangover, you now are doing the things you hate with more anger. You see no way out. Your bills must be paid.

If you are smart, eventually you will realize that this is your Matrix and you are Neo who has to break out of it. You will arrive at the conclusion that something has to change in your life. Then you will begin to look for a way to make it happen by searching for answers. Albert Einstein said, "We cannot solve our problems with the same level of thinking that created them." This simply means that you have to raise your level of consciousness to a higher perspective from which you can see your life as a whole. While many drugs can numb you to your depressing life in The Matrix, sacred plants can let you escape it. This is achievable when you use certain powerful plant teachers that can free your mind. Then you may get a glimpse of what it's like to be awake. But for the time being, you just want to solve your problems. And it's a really good start. Neo had to follow a White Rabbit to realize himself. I had to follow a green cactus. And you have to find your way.

There are many plants and many ways, not all of them for all people. We share our way with those who resonate with it. And for others who do not, keep looking until you find it. And when you do, you'll know it. It's a feeling. It's a knowing.

CHAPTER 19

THE CONVENIENCE OF A CITY IS INCONVENIENT TO YOUR SOUL

"The saddest aspect of life right now is that science gathers knowledge faster than society gathers wisdom."

— Isaac Asimov

Living in a box you can't escape from. Tracked, traced and watched. No, it's not a prison. It's the city you live in. I was born in a city and have lived in many. I never found happiness there. I felt that the noisy, polluted, restless, neurotic environment of a megapolis was harmful to my soul.

In every place I lived, I tried to find my refuge, where I could go and connect to Nature. In Ukraine, where I was born, we had a river and trees traversing our city. In Israel, where I grew up, we had hills in the north, deserts in the south, and the Mediterranean Sea, Dead Sea and Red Sea. In the United States, we had beautiful pine forests and lakes in Northern California. These were the places where I felt at peace. And of course, in Peru, we are living in the rural area of the Andes, the Sacred Valley of the Incas, surrounded by an inescapable beauty. These connections to Nature, books and psychedelics have kept me sane living in an insane world.

Growing up, I observed some kind of divide within myself. One part of me wanted to live a life of success and financial security and enjoy the best life has to offer, and another wanted to live a different kind of life. It was spiritual in essence. This part of me didn't find joy in material possessions, social status, etc. It simply didn't care. All it wanted was to be left alone, be quiet, be mindful and aware, read books, take psychedelics and think about life. To achieve that, I didn't need much money. In fact, the need for money was stealing this peace and joy from me. The society I

The Cactus of Sanity

lived in simply did not allow me to discover my passion. Instead it forced me to get a job and give the best of myself to an activity I actually hated doing.

What a world we are living in, I thought. Is that all there is for us to do here on this amazing living, breathing planet? Is this the purpose of this incredible, cosmic event, when I was conceived and born into this world? Though born with the ability to think and a tendency toward contemplation, I was forced to do mechanical jobs that would make a robot bored. My life force for a paycheck? What a trade! It felt so wrong. Struggling with societal pressure, more and more I found peace in psychedelics and reading. Looking at it now, I see all this previous hassle as necessary to enhance my spiritual search, which had started early on. The political climate of persecution we had to endure as Jews in Ukraine, the hardships of living in the socialist Soviet Union and the hassle and difficulties of being immigrants in Israel and later in the United States, all have contributed to the formation of that which today I call "me."

My character was forming in spite of religious and social pressure. The same was true for my life in the Fellowship of Friends cult in Northern California, a Fourth Way school for awakening, as they call themselves, where I spent six years.

All this I describe in my first book, which I recommend to anyone who has been following a fraudulent guru or an ideology, either on their own or as part of an organization. I'm sharing this now with one purpose: to help you see the good in the bad. The good, of course, is your opportunity to grow spiritually regardless of the circumstances, to learn to stand your ground, to learn to discern between right and wrong, moral and immoral, true and false, good or bad, and, above all, to be true to yourself. The bad is the environment you live in.

Of course, this doesn't at all mean that you have to suffer intentionally, and if you can change your circumstances, do it. Because this too enhances your willpower and thus contributes to your character. But if for some reason you can't, you still can make good use of what you have. All you need is to stop believing other people's versions of reality and figure out your own. You have to start believing yourself and your own feelings and build a relationship with the world from this inner space.

There is nothing normal or acceptable about the fact that we all have become slaves to the economic system we live in. There is nothing normal or acceptable about the fact that governments are corrupt and self-serving and see us as a

The Cactus of Sanity

means to their ends. There is nothing normal or acceptable about constant domestic or international conflicts that create tension, confusion and fear. The list goes on. But just as there is a collective reality, so there is a personal one, and because these are connected, we still can do something about the society we live in. It's not as futile as it seems. It's not all in someone else's hands, decided and determined.

A good psychedelic experience can take you out of it, to a whole other realm where you feel spiritually immune from this nonsense, a place where you simply feel YOU and are loving the feeling that leads to profound healing. Of course, there is set and setting to be considered, the type of substance or plant you decide to work with, and the proper guidance and a framework to put it all in. But if all the necessary conditions are fulfilled, you have a great opportunity to see through lies and illusions personally and collectively created. To see through them is to find liberation. It's the clarity and understanding that brings a sense of joy. Breaking the shackles, your mind simply flies like a bird, enjoying the flight.

It is a well-documented, historical fact that people lived in this way for thousands of years. Shamanic ecstasy was at the heart of every culture. All this has started to change fairly recently, considering the vastness of our human history, as organized religion took over about 3,000 years ago in the Middle East. Centralized power, centralized God; all controlled. No place for wonder, questions or to ponder; just belief. No more Divine you can touch, just a description of it in a book. Convenient for a few and limiting for the rest. A promise of the afterlife at the expense of your real life. The Glory of God after you're dead. Everything good is later, after and somewhere else, not where you are now.

This thought alone can trigger your personal awakening, if understood deeply. There is so much more to discover, learn and understand while we are alive that we barely have enough time to rest, as we feel the accelerating speed with which our lives are moving. The relentless clock of your life is ticking no matter what you do. Your life is a journey of learning and loving. There is no time to waste. Self-unawareness gives the illusion of immortality and lets you waste your precious time. Self-awareness shows reality as it is and keeps you focused.

There is no tension in Nature. There is no distress and no boredom. Nature is calm. It simply dwells in its own rhythm, the same rhythm that humans resonate with most. The city has another frequency. It is alien to Nature, alien to our

The Cactus of Sanity

spirit. We absorb this tension and go off balance, like one goes offline during a power outage. This causes frustration, irritability and anger, negative emotions that are depleting us spiritually and weaken us physically. Living in a city, you just don't have the time for anything that feeds your soul. Traffic, work, bills and news enslave you. You are tired, anxious, neurotic and fearful for what tomorrow may bring. I suggest you just leave your city for a few days. Go far beyond the city limits and your prejudices and see how people live in the rural areas. Talk to them. Ask them questions. Get the feel of their lives. This in itself can be a healing experience that can open new doors. I have traveled enough to confirm this to be true. They are connected to their land, which serves as their source for healing and peace. These people will survive the societal collapse that will look like an apocalypse to people living in the cities.

We live in the Sacred Valley of the Incas, Peru, in a small Andean town that has a few thousand families. It looks primitive from the outside, and yet I have everything I want and need in my life, plus much more.

I have freedom to be me. No pressure to be someone I'm not. I'm glad that my children are growing up here, on the land, among the mountains and other children who still play outside, not glued to their phones. We see sunrises and sunsets from our house. We see full and new moons. We see an infinite number of stars and the Milky Way.

The Cactus of Sanity

Sergey Baranov

The Cactus of Sanity

We wake up with birds, and we go to sleep with the magical sounds of crickets. We breathe clean mountain air, we eat non-GMO food, we drink fluoride-free water. We decide whether or not to vaccinate our children. We work with sacred plants, which are legal where we live. We live and we love, and we help others find their path in life. None of this would be possible if I chose to be a part of city life in the United States, fooled by its convenience and a false sense of prestige.

In *PATH, Seeking Truth in a World of Lies*, I share the story of having a relationship with a woman from San Francisco. She wanted me to marry her and live a zombie life there. I wanted to live in Peru and build my life around the sacred medicine, which I did, and which led me to my happiness. Looking back now, I feel a sense of horror thinking that I could have made the wrong choice and betrayed myself by staying with her. My life would have been ruined. My spirit would have been destroyed. For her my life in Peru was madness, for me madness is her life in San Francisco.

Technological advances also advance the existential void, a feeling of emptiness that we are trying to fill with stuff. We get tired of an old gadget and buy a new one, while thinking that a new iPhone will satisfy the inner void. If you take an aerial view of Apple headquarters, located at One Apple Park Way in Cupertino, California, you will see a circular building. Nicely built, with glassy walls, it provides a space for a few thousand employees to run within its walls like a hamster runs in a wheel — an iWheel that keeps millions of customers running with them in the same direction. New technology is a drug for many people who suffer from an existential void. Others prefer street drugs, alcohol and porn, which all serve as short-term antidepressants with long-lasting negative consequences. The newly formed habits become addictions, which only exacerbate the problem by suppressing the symptoms of a sick soul. This is exactly when one needs to start looking inside oneself and identifying the problem, so that it can lead to healing.

But things are actually getting worse. A brave woman named Rosa Koire speaks fearlessly and clearly about Agenda 21, a political agenda for the 21st century and a blueprint for human enslavement, in her book *Behind the Green Mask: U.N. Agenda 21*. If you familiarize yourself with it, you will find my tone to be too soft and not urgent enough. The plan is to put everyone into fully programmed smart cities, where you will be watched, traced and controlled every moment, inside your house and out. It will be like living in a nice jail; no freedom, no privacy. An Orwellian dystopian future has been drawn up for you and is already being implemented. And if you can't see it, it doesn't mean it can't see you. It is time to take action and decide what kind of future you want to have for yourself and your family.

Political decisions concern all of us, and in the U.S., Americans have a Constitutional right to express their concerns. Research the rights of the First Amendment, which are now under attack in the United States. Americans, an attack on your Constitution is an attack on you. Your Constitution is your only shield against tyranny. When it gets shredded, your civil liberties evaporate, and you can easily imagine what follows. Speaking up and speaking out is what's needed most today. Silence is a good meditation to practice in the mountains, so you can hear the echo of eternity passing through you. But to remain silent when you witness an injustice is both morally and spiritually wrong. This injustice is done to all of us as we speak, to the normal, law-abiding people who just want to live their lives peacefully and see their children grow. If we don't stand up for what's right, our children will inherit a toxic world run by psychopaths whose laws and rules will make life not worth living.

As I already said, our personal and collective reality are connected and the time we live in requires all of us to be politically aware. It is not what I would like to spend my time on, but this is what everyone needs to do today. A spiritual awakening is simply incomplete if it's exclusive. It's not an awakening at all, but a delusion, in which many gurus dwell; a self-made bubble in which they find their escape from reality. If your guru or teacher is not concerned about what's happening in the world and where we are heading as human species, I suggest you look elsewhere, for he or she is asleep.

As Ralph Waldo Emerson remarked in "Self-Reliance":

The Cactus of Sanity

"Society never advances. It recedes as fast on one side as it gains on the other. It undergoes continual changes; it is barbarous, it is civilized, it is Christianized, it is rich, it scientific; but this change is not amelioration. For everything that is given, something is taken. Society acquires new arts, and loses old instincts." He saw it 180 years ago, at the beginning of the industrial revolution. How relevant it is today.

CHAPTER 20

INDIVIDUALITY VS. THE COLLECTIVE

"To be yourself in a world that is constantly trying to make you something else is the greatest accomplishment."

— Ralph Waldo Emerson

What are you if your mind does not belong to you? If your thoughts are easily influenced by others? If your opinions are formed by the collective? If you don't have the strength to stand against the crowd with your own view? What is the point of being at all if there is no sovereign "you"? All religions, sects and cults are based on absorption of self into the collective. All as one, one as all. This approach only works in a battlefield, when an army is getting ready for combat. But living your life, learning and growing through this human experience, needs an opposite approach, and the battlefield is in your mind. You are one soldier against an army of collectivism. Submit and die spiritually, or be yourself and taste the taste of inner freedom. If you don't control your mind, someone else will.

The Cactus of Sanity

Individuality is the spiritual spine that defines our interface with the world. It's like a "soul print." Individuality is an antidote to collectivism and mind control. There are plenty of examples in history when political regimes demanded absolute obedience and submission. Having an opinion that might contradict the accepted narrative can be dangerous. In totalitarian regimes, such people are called dissidents, people who dare to challenge an established doctrine, policy or institution.

In the Soviet Union, this term was ascribed to people who criticized the practices or the authority of the Communist Party. These were intelligent people who stood and spoke against tyranny, wrote and distributed non-conformist literature. Dissidents were simply against oppression. The official narrative was to make these people look bad in the eyes of the public and prevent support from growing. They were painted as people who opposed society when, in fact, they were opposing an oppressive regime for the good of society. A primary element of dissident activity in the USSR was to inform the public about the violation of laws and human rights. People who can articulate problems and make other people think have become dissidents by default. The intellectuals who criticized the Communist regime became detractors and enemies of the state. Religion was condemned and banned as well, since it undermined the sole authority of the party. To speak for human rights or to support freedom of expression was to question the very basis of Marxism-Leninism and the legitimacy of the party's rule.

Bolshevik policy made a strong and continued effort to eliminate political opposition. Vladimir Lenin believed that literature and art were dangerous to the ideology of the Communist party if they were not controlled, but useful if exploited for ideological and political purposes. As a result, the party rapidly established control over all print, newspapers, books and libraries. Censorship was big in Soviet Russia. Suppression of newspapers, initially described as a temporary measure, became permanent policy, followed by mass arrests and deportations of professors, scientists, Kadets, Socialist Revolutionaries, Mensheviks, and Nationalists. Thus, a great purge of intellectuals began in Russia. Perceiving the growing tyranny of the Communist state, many writers emigrated and continued their criticism on the new Russian government from abroad. Being helpless to stop these intellectual attacks, the Soviet state denied all further emigration from Russia. Hence, the Iron Curtain covered Soviet Russia for the next 70 years.

The Cactus of Sanity

The majority of intellectuals and artists felt betrayed by their idealistic belief that revolution would bring a free society. Their disappointment did not surprise Lenin. After effectively using them to overthrow the previous Tsarist regime, he then saw them as political rivals who could cause an uprising in the future. Lenin decided to eliminate them. In 1928, the Central Committee assumed full control over literature and enforced new rules. Only those publications and exhibitions that promoted socialism were allowed; any piece of literature or art that did not contribute to the building of the socialist state was banned. The party removed writings from libraries that it did not view as politically correct. Stalin, Lenin's successor who took over the Soviet Union in the mid-1920s, asserted that art should be used to shape society in the way determined by the Communist party. As a result, artists and intellectuals, as well as political figures, became victims of the Great Terror of the 1930s. Authors whose works even appeared to be critical of the Soviet regime were persecuted and prosecuted. People were declared enemies of the state and imprisoned, or locked in insane asylums. Among those harassed and persecuted were world-renowned artists and scientists, including Nobel Prize winners Boris Pasternak, who was forced to refuse his prize; Aleksandr Solzhenitsyn, an outspoken critic of the Soviet

Communist ideology who was sentenced to eight years in a labor camp and then internal exile for criticizing Josef Stalin in a private letter; and Andrei Sakharov, who was expelled from the Academy of Sciences and internally exiled to a closed city. The persecution of intellectuals persisted throughout the whole Soviet period and is still present today.

During the war against Nazi Germany, artists were encouraged to infuse their works with patriotism and to direct them against the enemy. However, with the victory in 1945, the repression against deviation from party policy returned. Freedom of press and expression was brought to Russia by Mikhail Gorbachev, whose policy of 'glasnost' resulted in the abandonment of Marxist-Leninist ideology and a loss of legitimacy for the party. The Soviet Russia collapsed and its oppressive Communist regime failed. The remains of the regime persisted through time of perestroika, but it lost its grip over the masses.

The point I'm trying to make here is that individuality always has been and will be viewed by the status quo as a rival to its existence. Individuals have the power to resist and disobey orders that the masses blindly follow. Collectivism, an ideology hostile to individualism, can only prevail in oppressed society. China and North Korea are the classic

The Cactus of Sanity

modern examples. Privacy and freedom of speech, necessary conditions for exercising individualism, are the first things totalitarian regimes target. The eradication of individuality is a central theme of all dystopian literature. As George Orwell writes in his classic book, *1984*, collectivism wants "a nation of warriors and fanatics, marching forward in perfect unity, all thinking the same thoughts and shouting the same slogans…three hundred million people all with the same face."

But individualism is not a political stance that a person adheres to, although often it expresses itself as such. It is rather a character trait and a lifestyle. Its main principle is self-reliance. It always felt right for me to be me. It is vastly more difficult, if not entirely impossible, to control and indoctrinate individuals. My favorite individualist is Emerson, who wrote on the subject in a way that greatly resonates with me. In his excellent essay, "Self-Reliance," he stresses the importance of believing your own thoughts and feelings. He begins his essay with a passage from "Epilogue to Beaumont and Fletcher's Honest Man's Fortune," a tragicomedy written by Nathan Field, John Fletcher, and Philip Massinger, written in 1613 and published in 1647, referring to its lines as an "admonition which sentiment instils more value than any thought they may contain." "The soul," he says, "always hears an admonition in such lines, let the subject be what it may."

He continues by suggesting that a "man should learn to detect and watch that gleam of light which flashes across his mind from within, more than the lustre of the firmament of bards and sages." This urgency to trust yourself and your own experience is in fact an essential teaching of Huachuma medicine that prevails over any other ideas, regardless of how deep they might appear to the wandering mind. The power of Huachuma is in bringing you back to yourself, to your senses. He says, further:

"In every work of genius we recognize our own rejected thoughts: they come back to us with a certain alienated majesty. Great works of art have no more affecting lesson for us than this. They teach us to abide by our spontaneous impression with good-humored inflexibility then most when the whole cry of voices is on the other side. Else, to-morrow a stranger will say with masterly good sense precisely what we have thought and felt all the time, and we shall be forced to take with shame our own opinion from another."

Have you ever experienced hearing something from other people that you yourself have thought about but didn't trust

The Cactus of Sanity

enough to accept as truth? But when you heard others say it, you agreed wholeheartedly. It sure happened to me more than once, especially while reading. The problem is that neither religion nor the education system are teaching us this virtue. We grow up mistrusting ourselves while giving authority to others. To be dismissive of one's own self is a crime committed against one's spirit. It leads to lack of self-esteem and can form a submissive personality that will be subservient to others. It is a road that leads to bullying and abusive relationships that make one feel useless, unless one places him or herself at other people's disposal. Submissiveness will make you live your life with lowered head and take what you are not willing to accept. To break away from this humiliating state requires awareness and strength, both found in the Huachuma experience in abundance.

Emerson continues:

"He dismisses without notice his thought, because it is his. In every work of genius we recognize our own rejected thoughts: they come back to us with a certain alienated majesty. Great works of art have no more affecting lesson for us than this. They teach us to abide by our spontaneous impression with good-humored inflexibility then most when the whole cry of voices is on the other side. Else, to-morrow a stranger will say with masterly good sense precisely what we have thought and felt all the time, and we shall be forced to take with shame our own opinion from another."

"Trust thyself: every heart vibrates to that iron string," Emerson writes encouragingly. Socrates said, first, "Know Thyself," which seems to be the right order of things. In order to trust yourself you have to know yourself, otherwise who is there to be trusted? And in order to know yourself you have to be yourself. By being yourself you get to know yourself and therefore trust yourself. This simple guidance is profound and can transform your life.

Emerson adds: "These are the voices which we hear in solitude, but they grow faint and inaudible as we enter into the world. Society everywhere is in conspiracy against the manhood of every one of its members. Society is a joint-stock company, in which the members agree, for the better securing of his bread to each shareholder, to surrender the liberty and culture of the eater. The virtue in most requests is conformity. Self-reliance is its aversion. It loves not realities and creators, but names and customs.

Whoso would be a man must be a nonconformist. He who would gather immortal palms must not be hindered by the

The Cactus of Sanity

name of goodness, but must explore if it be goodness. Nothing is at last sacred but the integrity of your own mind. Absolve you to yourself, and you shall have the suffrage of the world. I remember an answer which when quite young I was prompted to make to a valued adviser, who wanted to import me with the dear old doctrines of the church. On my saying, What have I to do with the sacredness of traditions, if I live wholly from within? my friend suggested, — 'But these impulses may be from below, not from above.' I replied, 'They do not seem to me to be such; but if I am the Devil's child, I will live then from the Devil.' No law can be sacred to me but that of my Nature.

Good and bad are but names very readily transferable to that or this; the only right is what is after my constitution, the only wrong what is against it. A man is to carry himself in the presence of all opposition, as if everything were titular and ephemeral but he. I am ashamed to think how easily we capitulate to badges and names, to large societies and dead institutions. Every decent and well-spoken individual affects and sways me more than is right. I ought to go upright and vital, and speak the rude truth in all ways. If malice and vanity wear the coat of philanthropy, shall that pass?"

This is the essence of a spiritual warrior. A spiritual warrior does not look for war. He wants peace, but he is courageous and always ready to fight for his truth. This sentiment is well aligned with my Ayahuasca, Huachuma and Peyote teachers in Peru and Mexico. That's what medicine is doing best, purifying your heart and making you feel alive and truthful. It helps you accept yourself as you are and live your life from a place of self-confidence and strength. You live with compassion for the weak and sick and disdain for oppression and evil, that which enslaves the human body and spirit. This is the essence of shamanic teaching I was exposed to by Don Howard Lawler. I continue my work in this spirit.

"Individuality" means the character, self-respect, and principles by which individuals live their lives. They find joy in human connection as much as they find peace in solitude. Being alone with their own thoughts is medicine to them. Individuality is the first thing that gets attacked in totalitarian regimes, prisons, the military, and religious sects and cults. Individuality is the uniqueness of each person that gives a meaning to his or her existence. No one else can live your life for you. Only you can. No one else can be you.

Huachuma can help you actually realize and feel that you are fulfilled by being you, and this fulfillment is what actually matters. It's the feeling of immense freedom. To be your true, authentic self is to be free. This is what individuality means to me, to be indivisible within myself. To be one with myself. As Emerson says, "by doing your work you reinforce yourself".

Gurdjieff said, "if you want to lose faith, make friends with a priest." This seems to be in line with Emerson's sentiment. The concept of individuality played an important role in Gurdjieff's teaching. He claimed that individuality is a result of the work on oneself, something we develop, not inherit. I joined the Fourth Way partly because I wanted to develop it. But in the Fellowship of Friends cult, individuality was absorbed into the collective and made a part of the greater machinery that was using me, not working for me. I share my six years spent in "The Work" in my first book. Only later, when I was fortunate to find Huachuma cactus, I was finally able to connect the dots for myself. Huachuma has shown me another way, through experiencing myself as I am. A way of love, not of endless struggle.

If I wanted to become a guru and build a following, I would call it a Fifth Way, a way of direct experience. But this will never happen. I am allergic to gurus. My inner guru is the only one I listen. Being yourself is true freedom. You are free from other people's expectations and opinions. Exchanging yourself for a role means losing yourself in the process and wearing a mask, pretending to be something you are not. How imprisoning this must feel. Do not allow others to define your life. Do it yourself.

To be fair, this was a lesson I received from Ayahuasca when I came to Peru for the first time in 2005. She freed me from the burden of other people's opinions of me. Friedrich Nietzsche says it best:

"The individual has always had to struggle to keep from being overwhelmed by the tribe. If you try it, you will be lonely often, and sometimes frightened. But no price is too high to pay for the privilege of owning yourself."

CHAPTER 21

SELF-CONSUMING CONSUMERISM

"The man in the street does not know a star in the sky. The solstice he does not observe; the equinox he knows as little; and the whole bright calendar of the year is without a dial in his mind. His note-books impair his memory; his libraries overload his wit; the insurance-office increases the number of accidents; and it may be a question whether machinery does not encumber; whether we have not lost by refinement some energy, by a Christianity entrenched in establishments and forms, some vigor of wild virtue."

— Ralph Waldo Emerson, "Self-Reliance"

Jeff Bezos, the founder of Amazon, made a disturbing observation in one of his speeches. He said that people are divinely discontent. "You give them the best service you can, they love it, but they always want a little bit more." Bezos has seized the opportunity to use this spiritual void to his advantage and create a multinational tech giant that can deliver anything except divine contentment.

People from ancient times tried to understand themselves and their place in the Universe. Those who were thoughtful spent life in contemplation. They saw through the mirage of possession and titles, prestige and the ego. They retreated into that which they thought was timeless. They tried to become divinely content. As a result of this search for true happiness that wasn't material, they developed different ways to achieve spiritual fulfillment. And this great social equalizer was available to the poor, making them rich without having possessions. In fact, the poor became richer than the rich, since the rich always wanted to become richer, while the poor were simply self-content. Their stomachs were empty, and this caused physical discomfort, but their hearts were full, and their being was filled with a spiritual presence that compensated for the physical pain. They were seekers of truth and meaning in life, something that was real and worth doing. Taught by observation and common sense, practical wisdom was gained by life experience. Their daily bread was the daily guidance that didn't fall from the sky but was found within themselves. This is not at all to promote poverty as a solution. Poverty is a limiting factor and a slavery from which we all should be free. We can travel, learn and do more with money, as long as we see it as the means to an end, not the end for its own sake.

The Cactus of Sanity

They were us a long time ago. We share with them something that is never changing. Centuries or millennia pass; only the personal and cultural customs are different. Today, perhaps we are even emptier inside than people in ancient times. We have plenty of gadgets, but we don't have peace. With have money but we are not happy. We live in big cities, detached from the land. We don't see stars, we don't smell grass. We are glued to our screens, where most of our life happens. This lifestyle makes the soul suffer, and we try to buy it toys to calm it down; goods and gadgets as pain killers for the soul. Is there another way? A way that allows us to look inside and see the void and fill it with what truly matters? And when we do it, we realize that a lower price, faster shipping and an easier shopping just can't do it for us. The inner depth can only be reached with a spiritual experience that does not arrive in a package. A feeling of being fully alive comes from the experience of being fully alive. This can be only achieved under certain conditions.

Both religion and science create a culture of consumerism that trains us from early on to look for the sacred and the good outside of ourselves. They enhance idolatry and dependency while reducing self-reliance. The harm of packaged spirituality and improved technology might be greater than its good.

As Emerson said, "Nothing can bring you peace but yourself. Nothing can bring you peace but the triumph of principles." The set of values you base your life on is what brings you happiness. I place value in love for my family. This makes me happy as a human. I place value in direct spiritual experience, I work with Huachuma medicine. This brings me spiritual contentment. I place value in self-expression and creativity, I write books and make films. This brings fulfillment. I use technology to do it. And this is great. But this technology is under my control, it doesn't try to outsmart me or threaten my existence.

We are now sold on futuristic smart cities where we would be presumably happy commanding the lights in the room to turn off and on, a coffee machine to brew us coffee and a robot assistant to bring luggage down to the car. We are told that merging our brains with the machines to keep up with Artificial Intelligence will make us happy. But this is just another lie. A planned city with planned life, what boredom! A place where there is no more wonder, excitement or thrills, risk or uncertainty, no opportunity for personal growth. Only Google, which decides what you eat, think, feel and do.

The Cactus of Sanity

What a nightmare that is! It's a suicidal path. My decision-making process is what formed my character and made me be me. If A.I. takes this away, we will be growing without the ability to form our character, and without character we will be sheeple, drugged, confused and submissive. We can already see this happening today with the excessive influence on society of pharmaceuticals, pop culture and mainstream media.

While some look up to psychics who shake in epileptic seizures or listen to gurus and preachers in white robes, others simply observe the world with open eyes. It is the same world we see every day going to work, yet seeing it through a trance-like state maintained by certain cultural forces, thus preventing us from seeing naked reality.

John Carpenter demonstrated this reality in his movie *They Live*, which he wrote and directed in 1988. Ostensibly a science fiction/horror film, it shows a world in which the ruling class are an alien species, concealing their appearance under human form. Their true, hideous faces and ruthless manipulation of human society can only be revealed through special sunglasses, devised by an underground resistance. These fresh eyes also exposed subliminal messages embedded in the cultural landscape, demanding that we OBEY, CONSUME and CONFORM.

Leaving the notion of aliens to sci-fi, we do truly live beneath such a deceptive veil. The cultural hypnosis remains rather vivid to those wearing the actual "sunglasses" readily available to all — plant medicine. Besides the growing mechanisms of societal control, as portrayed decades ago in George Orwell's *1984* and Aldous Huxley's *Brave New World*, there is another theme that becomes apparent the moment you put on the sanity lenses. You begin to see the rise of mental illness and the legitimization of insanity. Political correctness is often applied as a tool for coercion. People are used as pawns in social experiments, unwittingly herded together as a doped, human shield against sanity. Psychology misused can become a psychological bioweapon, targeting people from within to turn them against themselves and others. This zombification is happening on a grand scale right now, and the tools with which to do it are becoming more powerful. The forces behind this are a whole other question, but the fact that our modern world is nurturing madness with increasing precision is obvious.

The conquest of the organic world is brutal, like the conquest of America by the Spaniards in the 15th century. Conquest is

The Cactus of Sanity

rarely a peaceful event, and it is exactly what I see happening with the development of A.I. 500 years ago the people of Peru had a choice to either accept a new faith and the new rulers from Spain or be killed. Not much of a choice, after all. Today, we are told that we are facing a similar choice as human society: to either accept the new faith of Technocracy or to be obsolete and starve to death. But this is just another lie. If we have made it so far in a human form, why can't we continue? Perhaps we need a computer to calculate the ever-growing national debt, but an intuitive heart is all we need to live, love and learn. History repeats itself again; only the setting and costumes are different.

The Starlink is a SpaceX project intended to build a constellation of thousands of small, mass-produced satellites in low Earth orbit and, working in combination with 5G ground transceivers, is supposed to provide faster internet. Certainly, it can be used that way; however, and at the same time, it can be used for total surveillance. It will cover every inch of the Earth's surface. Wikipedia says SpaceX also plans to sell some of its satellites for military, scientific, or exploratory purposes. Governments' exploration of your life, for example, fits well into this purpose. Their curiosity about our lives seems to be boundless. But if *The Terminator's*

"Skynet" is not enough, the Neuralink, another Elon Musk invention, can also have a dual purpose. It is a microchip implant in your brain that interfaces between humans and A.I. He claims it will ensure that humanity will be able to keep up with A.I. He also believes that a brain-chip will be the ultimate solution for people who suffer from disabilities and neurological disorders. A noble cause to pursue on the surface, but it's a two-way street. Just as a signal can be sent from the human mind to a computer, a signal can be sent from the computer to the mind. I don't doubt Musk's intention to serve humanity; the problem is that his creation can be misused and abused by other people. An engineer finds excitement in his invention, but the Devil might hide in the intention. The temptation to use this technology for mind control by the government or commercially by corporate interests might be simply too great to resist. Just imagine your life if thoughts were implanted in your mind, and you thought they were yours. You would start buying things you didn't want and doing things you wouldn't be doing otherwise. To me it looks like a techno-dystopian future that even George Orwell could not imagine. Syncing bio with tech is a process that might lead to the self-destruction of our species in the 21st century, which could be the last century for humanity if transhumanist madness isn't stopped. A war between men and machines is inevitable and it has already begun through automation. While automation and a robot-centered economy will make life easier for a few, it will make life impossible for the many. I wouldn't even mind this if the technology and push for innovation were not invasive, if the choice were left to people to follow different paths. But the truth of the matter is that it will be forcing all of us to adapt and change in ways many of us don't want.

The best way to predict the future is to invent it, so you can direct it into a self-fulfilling prophecy. Machines should be subordinate to humans, not the other way around. Each of us must make a firm decision about what path to follow in life. I don't want to be a cyborg, with a connection between my brain and the digital world. I want to be a human and maintain my connection to the natural world. For me, a video game will never replace Nature. Virtual is not my reality.

Elon Musk said that his dream is to die on Mars but not upon impact. To me, to die on Mars, away from Earth, would mean a double death. Earth, to me, is warm and big enough to live and die on. It's the planet I love. It's the place where my parents and grandparents are buried.

You cannot escape yourself, and if you feel empty on our beautiful Earth, you will feel even emptier on Mars or elsewhere. If all that is here is not enough for you to feel happy, how is all that is absent there will?

Each to his own. We see the world differently. He is a technocrat; I am a Nature lover. I want to be a human and die on Earth. I want to maintain my connection to Nature and to the Divine through it.

CHAPTER 22

HUACHUMA CACTUS VS. TECHNO-IDOLATRY

When was the last time you saw people talk to one another on the way to or from work? Take a moment to think about it. Whether you take a bus or train to reach your workplace, most of the time you see people glued to their phones, most likely including you. In fact, it has become so bad that people are now like drunks, walking into each other, bumping into walls, street lights, cars, falling into ditches and fountains while texting. Researcher Jack Nasar from Ohio State University says that there may have been about two million pedestrian injuries related to mobile phone use in 2010. A Pew Research Center survey[11] in mid-2012 found that 50% of cell owners say that they have been bumped into by another person who was distracted by using their cell phone. The "phone zombies" phenomenon has been looked at in other studies[12] as well. Not to mention the growing trend of selfie deaths[13]. If this were not so tragic, it would be hilarious!

Mobile technology has shifted from being a device for distant communication to a tool for mass hypnotism. The iPhone in the Western world today plays the role of the flute of the Indian fakir, whose sound hypnotizes the cobra. Your phone is that flute and you are the cobra. It keeps you in a constant trance while feeding you garbage news, negativity, propaganda and advertising. In modern American society, having a newer and better phone is prestigious. This form of techno-slavery is now as socially accepted as alcohol, another harmful stupefier that, like tech, creates the illusion of happiness. Technological idolatry is very naïve in its assumption that a collection of gadgets means liberation and freedom. Techno-idolatry has become a modern, transnational techno-religion, promoted by the media as the means to happiness. Billions of people online have created a cyberspace identity, which is highly vulnerable for manipulation and abuse. A lack of likes on Facebook or Instagram posts causes depression in teens and young adults and requires psychological treatment.

According to a recent study[14], Americans look at their phones 52 times a day, on average. Shocking! If they would look inside themselves as much, with an intention to see what's within them and self-reflect, their lives would transform. The problem, though, is that Western culture does not teach people this vital process of self-reflection. It is simply absent from the socio-cultural narrative. This is why Eastern spiritual traditions are helpful, for they point the way inward. Of course, plant medicine is a direct approach that leads to clarity and understanding of oneself and the world around. Still, reading the words of wise men of the past can be helpful. Learning to look inside is the only way toward healing and change.

Perhaps we can suggest a new term to be added to the psychiatric manuals: social media syndrome. The problem is that cyberspace, which is a generator of mass confusion, has assumed the role of teacher of humanity, thus becoming a source of knowledge to billions of people and a place from which they derive their philosophy for life. The constant rush for innovation creates a false notion that all that is new is better than all that is old. Let's take a moment to laugh at this. Recently, a friend of mine who went to South Korea on a business trip wrote to me to share his difficulties getting out of the bathroom. While on the toilet, he didn't know what button to press to flush it. A digital toilet had become a nightmare for my friend, who simply wanted to get done. 25 different buttons, all in Korean, made it impossible to conduct the simple act of flushing the toilet. Trying different ones, he got his butt blown with hot air, sprayed with warm water and germicide. To make his story more believable, he sent me pictures and video as he was trying to leave the cyborg toilet. He said, even to him, an MIT graduate, the innovation was too much to figure out. I laughed so hard

The Cactus of Sanity

that I woke my wife up, giggling at this digital tragicomedy. This was simply hilarious!

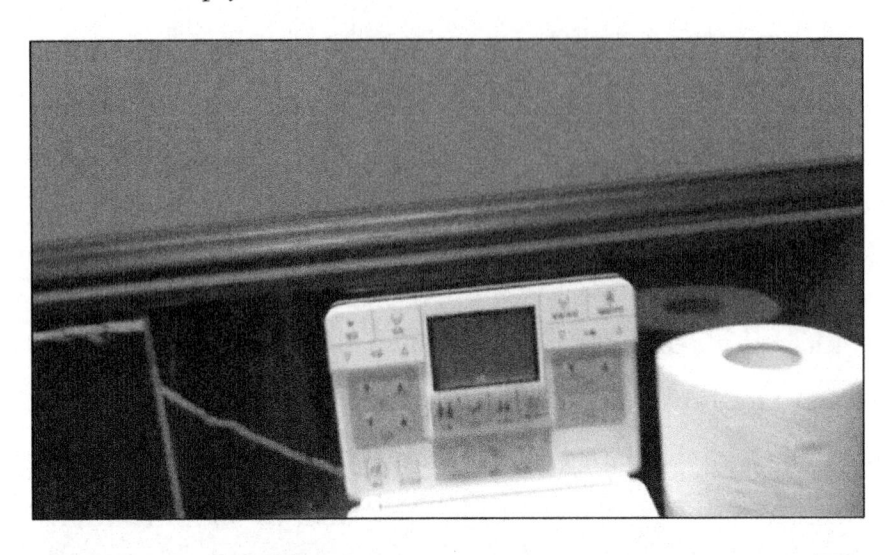

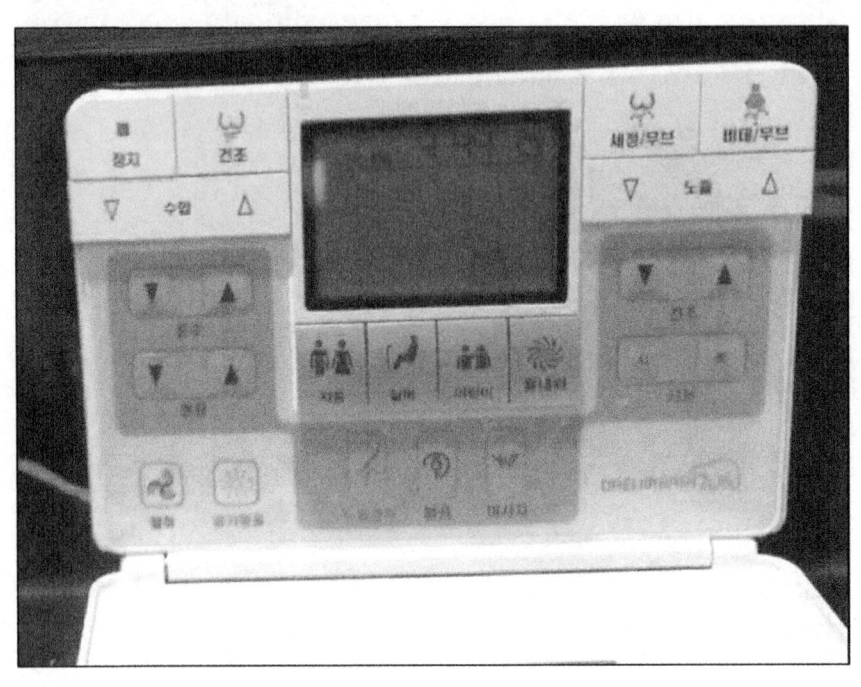

Sergey Baranov

The iToilet Dashboard

I would never install this "smart" toilet in my house so that it could make me look stupid. Trapped in a South Korean iToilet, my friend admitted that they have taken it too far. Personally, I choose the old-fashioned manual toilets, just as I choose old-fashioned personal communication with people. Even in this sense, older is obviously better. I have already explained my attitude towards technology earlier. I understand its value, and I use technology myself. But technology is my servant, not my God. I will never worship a machine, whether it is my cell phone, space shuttle or an iToilet.

There is a greater problem with the notion of innovation when it simply eclipses the old ways of living and thinking. It is impossible to discover in the popular thinking of our time any traces of profound ancient teachings. Cleverness is never wisdom. These vital teachings that we need in order to live our lives in the right way have been simply deemed old, irrelevant and void by the techno-digital culture. But constantly advancing technology comes with a heavy price of alienation from self and Nature. Tech culture is becoming the new fanaticism that can only offer a substitute for happiness, but never happiness itself. We even now have the

The Cactus of Sanity

cult of Apple, and people take pride in being part of it. The new gods, such as Google, Facebook and Twitter, are worshiped and feared for being deplatformed for politically incorrect speech. A digital hell has now been created; users are sentenced to Facebook jail for merely questioning the official narrative that is controlled from Silicon Valley, where social engineers have assumed the divine right to rule. For them technology means salvation. Greatly wired but deeply disconnected, we live our lives not realizing that this separation from ourselves and Nature is the root of our human suffering. Huachuma's sobering, problem-solving clarity is truly a blessing from Nature. But in much of the world it is banned by the powers that shouldn't be. The antidote for human madness is outlawed. What a sad, wrong truth! Meanwhile, human flesh consumption is being promoted by a behavioral scientist on TV[15] — speaking of insanity for a moment!

The good news is that this awful reality is only one way to engage with life. People in ancient times revered Nature for its healing powers. The plant kingdom is immense and is readily available to use. There are natural ways for healing that have proved to work over thousands of years. All true connections are rooted in our hearts, and sacred plants are here to show us what's in them. As if on a display, we can see our inner content and make the necessary changes in our lives, in order to provoke our inner capacity for good and ensure the flow of the healing energy available to us. Rewired and reset by the power and intelligence of sacred plants, we are able to unlock our higher potentials for creativity and conscious living. We have to make room within ourselves for spiritual connection. Higher states of consciousness are the necessary food for our souls, which are mostly malnourished and deficient from living in the modern world. The urge towards unity is coming from the depths of our spirit, which is a part of the Whole. Huachuma medicine is this Universal connector.

Benjamin Whichcote said that "good men spiritualize their bodies. Bad men incarnate their soul." This statement would make even more sense if we simply replace "good" and "bad" with "self-aware" and "unaware." Incarnated in technology, our spirit has fallen ill and is heading towards the emergency room. I found Huachuma medicine to be the answer to many questions and spiritual illnesses, which get solved in the greater clarity of the mind. This, of course, irritates the impotent, reductionistic scientists, who have become idolaters of scientific dogma and the atheistic view of life. To them, the spiritual realm is a hallucination, a place in some dark corner of the human mind where only delusional and mentally ill people dwell. To their limited spiritual perception and understanding, the intelligence of a plant deserves no attention, for, in their own minds, it doesn't exist. Ergo, both science and technology are moving backwards while sustaining an illusion of progress.

All this becomes clear when you embrace Huachuma medicine in the right way and allow yourself to see with your heart and mind. It is by the tranquility of the mind that we can transmute the false realities and pseudo-religions of the present and afterlife salvation of the future. Here and now is the only place and time where salvation is possible. From a lifelong spiritual search, I have found plant-based shamanism, Sufism and Zen Buddhism to be the ways that most stress the importance of living in the present moment. Huachuma medicine, in particular, is that messenger whose clear and direct message reaches the depths of one's heart.

There are many conceptions of salvation, and most of them are exclusively realized in a posthumous condition. The wide-spread belief in an external agent or agency must be abandoned, for it is the major block in taking our lives and destiny in our hands. From the Messiah of the ancient times to the alien ambassadors of the New Age, humanity has been and still is waiting for a God-like figure to descend from somewhere and save us all from our own ignorance and mess. This naïve and perhaps even irresponsible attitude towards life is perhaps the greatest obstacle to personal and collective change. All externalized forms of salvation must be internalized. Saving ourselves from our own ignorance is a good start.

The last recorded words of the Buddha were: "Decay is inherent in all component things. Work out your own salvation with diligence." Perhaps the greatest gift of Huachuma teaching is this very guidance toward yourself and your own salvation. It is the self-realization of the inner guru that Eastern literature predominantly speaks of. At any time of human history, this powerful ally would be a blessing. But today, with the rise of mental illness in the world, this kind of experience and connection is vitally important. The Buddha is right. You are your own savior.

As Mahayana Buddhism's *Sutra Alamkara* states: "Indeed, the saving truth has never been preached by the Buddha, seeing that one has to realize it within oneself." And this is perhaps the most important gift of Huachuma medicine. It allows you to do that, among other things. It simply opens your inner vision so you can see the illusory Nature of devouring pseudo-salvations such as materialism, technology, science and religion: the worship of analytical reason on one hand and superstitious beliefs and dogmas on the other. Huachuma can clearly show you that organized religion is just a collection of dogmas and is not a safe ship to board on a voyage across the ocean of life. The same is true for scientific materialism. Both boats have holes in them and both will sink on the way. The bottom line is that awakening is no longer a privilege of the few but a necessity of the many, and it is achievable under certain conditions.

Huachuma is a gentle veil-lifter you can trust. It turns on the light in your room, where you can see perfectly what's inside. In its bright, vibrant light, what was obscure now can be seen clearly. And just as you can see the disorder in your room when the light is on, so too in the light of Huachuma medicine, you can see the disorder in your life. Seeing leads to healing and change. Self-realization is the enlightenment of the Self. Become your own light. Don't look for an external refuge. This is a teaching you find in Huachuma cactus. And these are not merely words. It's what you feel, it's what you experience. And this experience is louder and clearer than any words.

I dedicated my second book, *The Mescaline Confession*, to the Huachuma cactus. This book is the light dose of my medicine. If you resonate with my words, you are ready to take the next step and experience Huachuma medicine with us in Peru. There is simply no more time for prejudices. The only time we have is for healing and regeneration. But of course, it comes only with learning, deep, sincere contemplation and fearless diving inside your own self.

Plant medicine shamanism is the way to go from here forward. Concepts like Heaven, Nirvana, Samadhi and Enlightenment won't take us far. If we don't find our spiritual roots, we will simply destroy ourselves and everything around us. What we need is a direct spiritual experience of Divine Union to transform our lives. This transcendent experience is the unifier that ensures mutual thriving. No amount of political and economic planning will get the job done until we find the connection with ourselves and Nature.

CHAPTER 23

A.I. AND THE SYNTHETIC REALITY: HORRORS AND HOPES FOR THE FUTURE

In my recent book, *The Mescaline Confession*, I wrote about a stark vision I received one day from the Huachuma cactus, warning of a future in which our own technology will devour us. It showed me a disturbing, dystopian future in which humanity was no longer in charge. It was on the verge of collapse. A species that had made it through millions of years of evolution, growing and learning, now faced extinction. Technology, the cactus told me, is not our God — it is our servant. Technology itself is a tool that is neither inherently good nor bad, but technology without wisdom is weaponized stupidity. It was such a dire, seemingly inescapable fate, that all my being yielded to sadness. What can be done? I silently asked. What was the solution to this big problem we ourselves are inexorably creating? The answer didn't come that day, but later I came to understand that the answer was already in my hands: It was plant medicine.

Recently, I stumbled upon a profound essay that echoed these revelations quite closely:[16] "Why the Future Doesn't Need Us," by Bill Joy, published in *Wired* magazine way back in April 2000. Primarily about the potential dangers of giving artificial intelligence, robotics and nanotechnology greater autonomy and control over their given roles, it also critiqued the rabid transhumanist movement, a giddy group, hell-bent on merging our bodies and minds with computer technology in a quest for god-like, never-ending life. Once quite rudimentary, transhumanism has come a long way, attracting devotees seeking to "improve humanity" (but really just their own) by embedding and/or replacing their bodies more and more significantly with tech, making us "better" and even — their primary goal — "immortal." The transhumanist agenda's hysterical craving for eternal life is more likely an insane drive toward what, I believe, will be a post-human future in which cold calculation will rule the world, pushing true humanity to extinction. Perhaps nothing more than the same old fear of death is the driving force behind this obsession. The idea of uploading human consciousness into a computer in search of immortality is a digital analogue of the religious belief in a heavenly afterlife. The only difference: their version of Heaven is virtual.

The lure of immortality has entranced humanity for thousands of years, but we have always possessed countless ways to attain it. Many have, in fact, achieved immortality throughout human history; Classical Greek philosophers, the builders of ancient Egypt, the musicians and writers of medieval ages in Europe and many others have acquired it by making a lasting dent in human history, influencing the way we live and think today. They have become immortals in our minds and culture. On what seems a smaller scale, but I think no less significant, our deceased grandparents and parents are continuing to live as long as we remember them. Today, however, with advances in science and technology, immortality has taken on new meaning. Taken literally, the pursuit for everlasting individual life is now running full steam in Silicon Valley, bringing my frightening vision closer to a reality.

The transhumanist desire to extend the body and mind with technology is actually a desperate attempt to compensate for a sense of incompleteness that in fact is illusory. Transhumanism wouldn't be a big concern if prominent tech people, such as the figurehead of the movement, Ray Kurzweil, were not involved. Obsessed with transhumanism, Kurzweil is a leading voice in futurism and development, having invented the digital scanner and made many accurate predictions about the course of computer tech. He has been employed by Google since 2012, as a director of engineering.

In his article, Bill Joy recounts an interaction with Ray in a hotel bar, where the latter gave him a partial pre-print of his then-forthcoming book, *The Age of Spiritual Machines* (1999). It outlined a utopia he foresaw — one in which humans gained near immortality by becoming one with robotic technology. Reading it, Joy's sense of unease only intensified; he felt that he understood the negative potential of this "utopia," and saw the probability of a bad outcome along this path.

An eminent computer scientist and co-founder of Sun Microsystems, where he served as chief scientist for over 20 years, Joy is no Luddite and states this very clearly. Indeed, he has contributed over many years to marked increases in the power of software, but this history only gives him a more personal sense of responsibility for the darker turns it might take. While expressing deep concern over the development of modern technologies, he raises important ethical questions that would be wise to consider today, similar in theme to those that the sacred cactus revealed to me that difficult afternoon in the Sacred Valley.

It seems unlikely, for example, that transhumanists have given much thought to what life would be without death. In my first book, I recounted my near-death experience in

The Cactus of Sanity

Mexico in 2008, during a peyote ceremony. Numerous deadly scorpion stings on my thighs took me very close to the precipice between life and death during the three hellish days that followed. I was dying during much of this time, giving me a deep insight into the vital, inextricable relevance that our inevitable death has to life. Death, I learned, is my friend: the overarching motivator to true living. Without death, I realized, we wouldn't seek to achieve the things that we do with the urgency that our brief existence in this world demands. Life's vibrancy is in fact dependent on its inescapable demise. Death makes us human.

Like Joy, I am no Luddite, but a line needs to be drawn. Technology is valuable but must be advanced with great caution. As I wrote in *The Mescaline Confession*:

"I need my phone because it helps me stay connected to my family. At the same time, it also connects me to the Matrix, with all its fear and madness. The lives of billions of people are brewing daily in my pocket. This, I thought, was the dark side of technology, which charms us with convenience, but in fact claims our mind. Convenience, I thought, was the Trojan horse allowing the virus to access our minds at virtually any time, a self-terminating virus meant to simulate life to destroy it."

The delusion of digital utopia provided by A.I. has raised concerns in many people, among them the firebrand technologist, Elon Musk, but his solution may lead to deeper problems. In a recent appearance on *The Joe Rogan Experience* podcasts, when asked about the danger of A.I., Musk responded that he had warned influential people, including then-US president Barack Obama, of the dangers inherent in advancing the technology — that it's the genie in the bottle. His warning, sadly, fell on deaf ears. This, he indicated, partly inspired the creation of his new company, Neuralink Neurotechnology, in order to develop an implantable brain-computer interface. Through symbiosis with artificial intelligence, Musk believes we might withstand the existential threat to humanity posed by unchecked A.I., enabling us to compete — or at least keep up — with our mysterious new silicon children. He believes that the merging of humans and machines is inevitable, saying that if we cannot stop it, we should join it. Joy asks in his article, "Given the incredible power of these new technologies, shouldn't we be asking how we can best coexist with them?" Musk's answer is to become, at least somewhat, more like them.

The Cactus of Sanity

But can this "can't beat 'em, join 'em" approach have a dark side? While Musk's Neuralink is apparently purely motivated and might have positive applications, the potentials for its abuse are vast and terrifying. With it, we are fast approaching a time where we will be able to order, for example, a pizza, by mere thought. Since Neuralink and its like will almost certainly come to know our unconscious better than we can, it will soon be able to present us with a pizza delivery we didn't even know we wanted! It will literally read our minds at depths of which we are rarely conscious. Just as the inventors of the wheel did not conceive of them rolling under the tanks that crushed life in Tiananmen Square, there are surely dire consequences that will stem from the optimistic invention of Neuralink and A.I., consequences of which we cannot presently conceive. Those that we can conceive of are bad enough! For example, as I write, people's expressed thoughts can and are being used against them, destroying their lives. A half-dazed, midnight tweet can ruin you. And here we are, fast approaching a time when all of our most private contemplations, conscious or not, will be available to the elites as weapons to be used against us. We are what we do, of course, not what we think. We have broad imaginations but are blessed with the moral ability to choose the ethical course of action.

Think about that, honestly... As morally upright a human being as you may be, have you not had thoughts that, if exposed, might have ruined your relationships or social standing? Wishing your neighbor ill, for example, for playing music too loud. Many if not all of you have thought such "evil" things, at some time, under certain circumstances. How many more such dark ideas might you be suppressing beneath your consciousness? As it advances, Neuralink might learn to see them, regardless. It would be foolish to think we could keep our Neuralink just between us and our PC. Even now, your phone transmits all manner of information, from your very location to your favorite color to your heart rate. Perhaps as soon as 2025, five years from now, our least compassionate "superiors" will possess a more powerful tool to find and prosecute "thought crime" than Orwell dared to imagine in his *1984*. Your criticism of government policies will no longer have to be expressed to have consequences. You just think about it, and the signal reaches the thought police.

This rather depressing sentiment made me think of another strategy: What if we humans form a resistance and collectively reject the notion itself? I myself have no desire whatsoever to install any kind of silicone implant in my body in order to function "better" and compete with my calculator. This is why

The Cactus of Sanity

I have the calculator, so it can do the calculation for me. Most certainly I don't want to become it. Rather, I prefer to spend time in Nature and use sacred plants, which are the best link we have to both organic life on Earth and the cosmic mind. The more I do it, the less I want to become a cyborg. Plant technology guides us toward our highest potential.

Transhumanism, to me, appears to be a kind of cosmic virus that, ironically, promises life extension but in fact threatens human life as we know it. What these people fail to realize is that our short time here already can and does lead to immortality of much greater value, that living and dying cannot be easily separated, and that ancient technologies for understanding the absolutely essential Nature of life and death have existed for millennia, upon the very ground on which we stand. Joy's piece has only become more relevant as we stampede toward the unknown consequences of bio-technological integration.

Thankfully, the earth has provided us with plant medicines, which are the perfect antidote to the cosmic virus. Human power structures, however, particularly in Western society, have made these psychoactive agents illegal. They banned the cure. Springing freely from the soil, plant medicines are the antibodies we need to combat diseases of the psyche. They contain the nutrients we need in order to enhance our spiritual immune system. With plant medicines we can embrace seemingly ephemeral, human life as it is. They can easily help us to understand clearly the error of the transhumanist course and steer away from it, avoiding the surrender of too much decision-making to heartless, glorified calculators in the name of our precious, temporary convenience. They teach us that it is mere egomania to attempt to literally live forever.

The more of us who experience the loving awareness provided by Huachuma, the stronger our collective sanity becomes. After countless years of spiritual human-plant connection — briefly paused by the rise of a relatively recent, consumerist machine — the plants are finally making their way back to the main stage. We can only spread the word and hope that they reach enough people before we spiral ever deeper into mechanistic notions of "improved" existence. I believe we may yet be shown the light before we are destroyed by our ever-increasing concessions to convenience. There is nothing convenient about the end of our beautiful species. We are fine just the way we are. We only need to realize it. The technology to do so is, and always has been, close at hand.

CHAPTER 24

ON MIND

"My religion consists of a humble admiration of the illimitable superior spirit who reveals himself in the slight details we are able to perceive with our frail and feeble mind."

— Albert Einstein

When I was a kid I was fascinated with the human body. When I was around 10 years old, on the way to the stadium where I practiced football, I would walk by a medical school that had a human skeleton that could be seen through a window, assembled in a standing position. I don't know why, but every day I stopped and looked at it, asking myself a question: What makes me be me? If I am that, those bones and flesh standing there lifelessly, what makes me alive? What animates this body and makes me feel a unique sense of self that could not be explained to others but is self-evident for me?

It was clear to a 10-year-old boy that there was more to a human being than just anatomy and its assemblage of organs. I knew myself in a way that I could not even explain to myself. I perceived myself as a self-aware presence of some kind, something that later I learned was called consciousness. How this assemblage of bones and flesh created this sense of being me, was and still is a mystery, not only for me but the leading neuroscientists in the world today. No one actually knows how lifeless particles create a human experience. Some researchers, faced with the problem of consciousness, have decided to reject the notion itself and thus assume that the problem is solved.

In his essay, "MIRROR NEURONS and imitation learning as the driving force behind 'the great leap forward' in human evolution,[17]" V.S. Ramachandran, Ph.D. in neurology from Trinity College at Cambridge University, contemplates puzzling questions about the evolution of the human mind and brain. One of the questions he asks is, why the sudden explosion (often called the "great leap") in technological sophistication, widespread cave art, clothes, stereotyped dwellings, etc. around 40,000 years ago, even though the brain had achieved its present "modern" size almost a million years earlier?

The hominid brain grew at an accelerating pace until it reached its present size of 1500cc about 200,000 years ago. Yet uniquely human abilities such as the invention of highly sophisticated "standardized" multi-part tools, tailored clothes, art, religious belief and perhaps even language are thought to have emerged quite rapidly around 40,000 years ago — a sudden explosion of human mental abilities and culture that is sometimes called the "big bang." If the brain reached its full human potential — or at least size — 200,000 years ago, why did it remain idle for 150,000 years? Most scholars are convinced that the big bang occurred because of some unknown genetic change in brain structure.

This is a very interesting question that I myself pondered for years. What caused such a dramatic and sudden change in human activity, which went against the forces of evolution? Natural selection only allows for those traits to remain that have survival value. What was the survival value in art 40,000 years ago when hunting and fishing occupied the day of those who wanted to live? Hunting and fishing have survival value but spending time creating rock art does not. In fact, it goes against the law of preservation of energy. You eat to gain energy to hunt, then rest so you can hunt again the next day. Why would you even have an impulse to decorate your cave with paintings? Same goes for dancing and music, none of which have survival value. Nevertheless, and in spite of the forces of natural selection, from around 40,000 years ago, these human traits appeared and evolved since.

The Cactus of Sanity

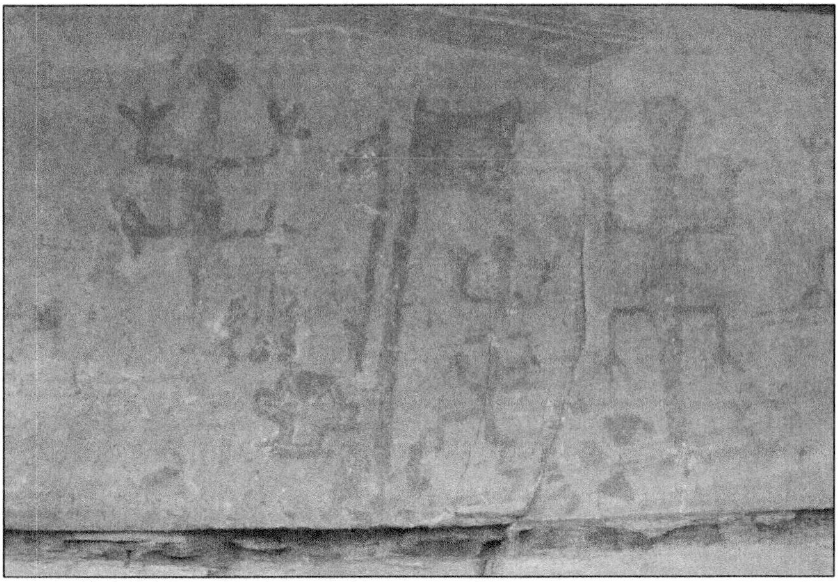

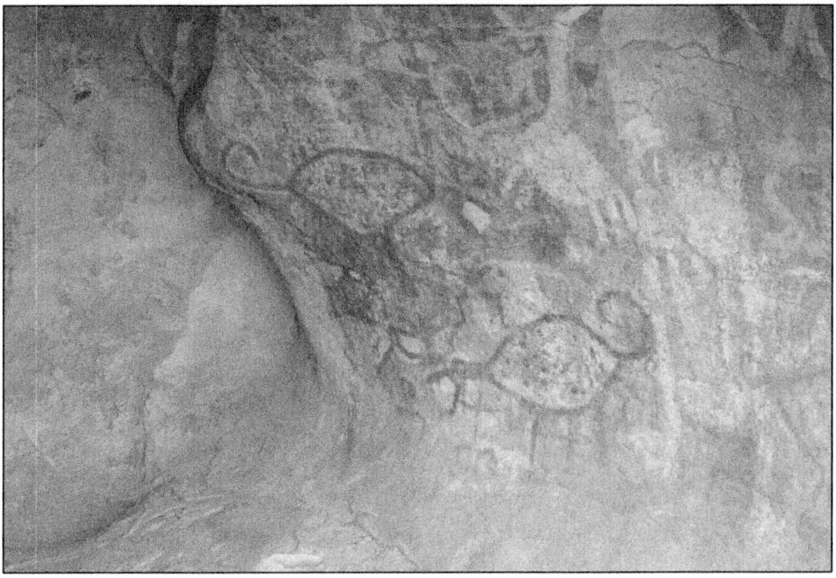

The Cactus of Sanity

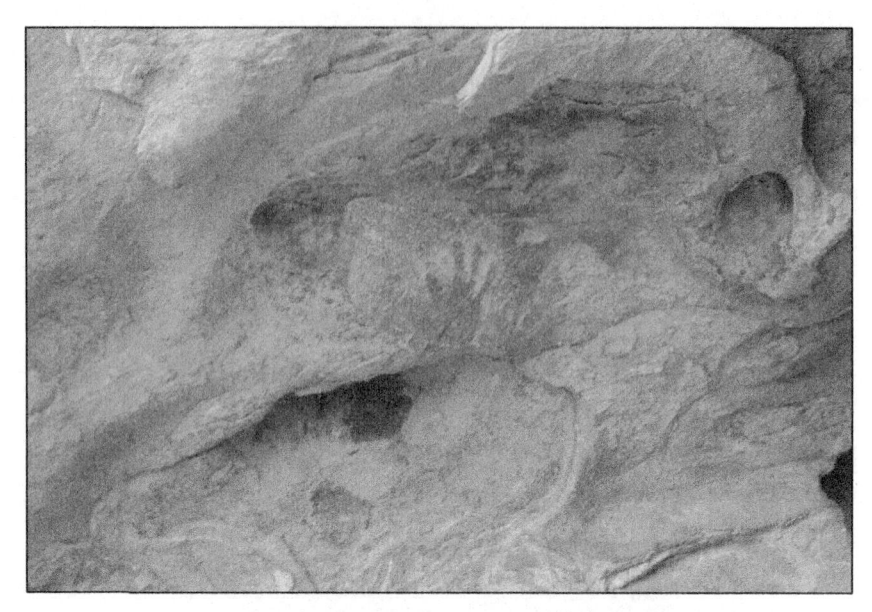

I pondered this question often during Huachuma ceremonies. The only reasonable explanation I could find for it is that the leap forward was possible due to men stumbling upon psychedelic plants, in much the way Terence McKenna promoted via his "stoned ape" theory, which was elaborated further by alternative history researcher Graham Hancock in his book, *Supernatural: Conversations with the Ancient Teachers of Mankind.* Such a dramatic experience in their minds could trigger an awareness that formed evolving human consciousness. With it, an impulse to make art as a form of self-expression came along. This could answer Ramachandran's question: Why did sophisticated tool use and art emerge only 40,000 years ago even though the brain had all the required latent ability 100,000 years earlier?[18] But what I find to be even more interesting is the fact that the plants were already there, fully formed, waiting for us. How did it occur that human physiology and psychology had receptors for the alkaloids that were in the plants that, upon intake, created a dramatic shift in perception with consequences on human evolution? This question might never be answered; however, I feel like just asking it still brings us closer to the mystery. The plants, as it seems, were waiting for us to evolve to a point when we were able to use them. It is quite obvious that neither Ayahuasca nor Huachuma, nor other plant teachers either, are growing for themselves. Their spiritual dimension becomes experiential only upon impact with human consciousness. In fact, they can only fully experience themselves in symbiosis with humans. Without us, they are just plants, not multidimensional beings. By the same token, we can experience our spiritual dimension by interacting with them.

However complex our brain and mysterious the phenomena of consciousness might be, baffling even the greatest minds throughout human history, there are still others who chose the reductionist approach to the problem and dismissed it altogether, in order to satisfy their scientific arrogance and ego.

Marvin Minsky, one of the founders of the transhumanist movement, said: "What magical trick makes us intelligent? The trick is that there is no trick. The power of intelligence stems from our vast diversity, not from any single, perfect principle." (*The Society of Mind,*[19] Chapter 30, Mental Models)

This is a classic materialistic view. The trick is that what makes us intelligent is consciousness, the elephant in the room that remains overlooked by the materialist view. Minsky, like any other atheist, materialist, reductionist scientist, failed to recognize himself in a mirror. He wrote books but died without being able to make a solid case for lack of consciousness in human beings. "Mind is what brains do," he said, but how? He had no answer. How mindless particles create a mindful experience remains a mystery to science.

Minsky further asserts that the concept of free will is an ancient myth refuted by modern science. The very essence of Gurdjieff's teaching was based on the concept of free will that, he says, exists in most people in a latent form but can be awakened by conscious effort. Minsky has observed only two forces governing our lives. First, the Cause, as he calls the rigid laws of nature, such as heredity and environment and Chance, what Gurdjieff referred to as to the Law of Accident.

"There is no room for a third alternative," writes Minsky. "We each believe that we possess an Ego, Self, or Final Center of Control, from which we choose what we shall do at every fork in the road of time. To be sure, we sometimes have the sense of being dragged along despite ourselves, by internal processes which, though they come from within our minds, nevertheless seem to work against our wishes. But on the whole we still feel that we can choose what we shall do. Whence comes this sense of being in control? According to the modern scientific view, there is simply no room at all for 'freedom of the human will.' Everything that happens in our universe is either completely determined by what's already happened in the past or else depends, in part, on random chance. Everything, including that which happens in our brains, depends on these and only on these: 1) A set of fixed, deterministic laws. 2) A purely random set of accidents. There is no room on either side for any third alternative. Whatever actions we may 'choose,' they cannot make the slightest change in what might otherwise have been -- because those rigid, natural laws already caused the states of mind that caused us to decide that way. And if that choice was in part made by chance -- it still leaves nothing for us to decide."

Determinism, an idea of a fixed future, has never appealed to my mind. I always felt that we are mentally equipped and have evolved in order to determine our own fate. *Magnum opus* ("the Great Work," in Latin) was an alchemical term describing a process of spiritual transformation and individuation. My life is a witness to the fact that heredity, environment and chance can be evaded by the making of conscious choices. My present is the result of that third alternative that Minsky claims does not exist.

Neither psychology, physics nor neuroscience can locate the mind in the brain. We know that it is there, but we fail to weigh it, measure and capture it on the screen. Nor can they locate a spirit in Nature or God in the Universe. Nature tells us that it is Divine, but we keep looking for God in the sky. I agree with Minsky when he says that there is always a room for doubt. The trick is, you have to know when to stop. Otherwise, you might begin to doubt your own existence and the existence of everything else. Eventually, it's where reductionism leads.

CHAPTER 25

WHO IS RICHARD DAWKINS FOR RICHARD DAWKINS?

"The finest emotion of which we are capable is the mystic emotion. Herein lies the germ of all art and all true science. Anyone to whom this feeling is alien, who is no longer capable of wonderment and lives in a state of fear is a dead man. To know that what is impenetrable for us really exists and manifests itself as the highest wisdom and the most radiant beauty, whose gross forms alone are intelligible to our poor faculties - this knowledge, this feeling ... that is the core of the true religious sentiment. In this sense, and in this sense alone, I rank myself among profoundly religious men."

— Albert Einstein

I find myself in a strange position that requires me to oppose atheist, reductionist science and its representatives, when, in fact, I was born atheist, grew up in the atheist environment and hold strong views against religious indoctrination. However, my attitude toward religion has been shaped by psychedelics, particularly mescaline, which is the active alkaloid in Peyote and the Huachuma cactus.

The real problem with Darwinism is that it is purely materialist. It seems that Darwin never asked himself a simple question: Who is looking? Who is actually looking at the phenomenal world? That of course would be a question for the mystic — not the scientist — and that is the difference between the two. Darwin's attention was never directed inwards, always outwards, focused on the physiology of man, as though it were only an assemblage of muscles and

The Cactus of Sanity

bones. While working hard to prove his theory of evolution, he was looking at the anatomical resemblances between a human and the anthropomorphic apes, while completely ignoring that which actually makes all the difference: the idea of consciousness, which some in the scientific world fiercely reject. Consciousness is the elephant in the room that our "luminaries of science" cannot find under the microscope, not realizing that what they are looking for is who they actually are, behind the microscope. That, of course, has been understood for millennia in the East by the mystics, sages, yogis, Sufis, Daoists and Buddhists — all of whom Darwin viewed as savages and brutes.

He viewed ancient shamanic traditions in a similar way. He speaks about the spiritual perception of the world as though a delusion of the primitive people:

"The tendency in savages to imagine that natural objects and agencies are animated by spiritual or living essences, is perhaps illustrated by a little fact which I once noticed: my dog, a full-grown and very sensible animal, was lying on the lawn during a hot and still day; but at a little distance a slight breeze occasionally moved an open parasol, which would have been wholly disregarded by the dog, had any one stood near it. As it was, every time that the parasol slightly moved, the dog growled fiercely and barked. He must, I think, have reasoned to himself in a rapid and unconscious manner, that movement without any apparent cause indicated the presence of some strange living agent, and that no stranger had a right to be on his territory."

— The Descent of Man, Charles Darwin

This quote shows us Darwin belittling the spiritual perception of the world by comparing it to a dog's defensive reflex. The metaphysical, spiritual realm, which cannot be measured by science, and yet can be experienced and observed by all, is completely absent in the Darwinian materialist worldview, whose representatives would deserve compassion if they weren't so arrogant.

The question arises: Can these people be cured?

The answer is yes, but only if they are willing to take a stiff drink of mind-blowing and soul-shaking plant medicine, which has the capacity to shake the materialist paradigm so profoundly that a perceptional shift will follow. Perhaps then, we could sit down and have a mature discussion about the war on consciousness, alternative medicine and spirituality that has been silently waged by the inquisitorial scientific establishment, run by people who are in fact in denial of their own existence.

I wish that Charles Darwin had searched for the link in physics between mind and matter with the same enthusiasm with which he searched for the connecting link between the man and apes. And I also wish he had realized, while looking for this link, that the act of looking itself was more important than anything he could ever find.

By the same token, I never would have thought that I would be the one opposing public intellectuals and academics like Richard Dawkins and others. Still, my vast experience with psychedelics demands that I do it. I will not offer a point by point analysis of an hour long discussion between Joe Rogan and Richard Dawkins on *The Joe Rogan Experience* podcast,[20] but although I agree with Dawkins about the silliness of some religious beliefs that have been presented as facts, his antagonistic approach to religious experience as a whole deserves a comment. Dawkins's main claim is that there is no God, there is no intelligent design and essentially there is no you.

Being myself a convert from atheism, I cannot imagine how a person can make such definite statements about God and the Nature of reality without having even one psychedelic experience. While he agrees that most of the world's religions appeared out of some sort of psychedelic experience, he discourages people from trying psychedelics for themselves. His stance is based on advice from his father's cousin, whom Dawkins thinks was the person who introduced Huxley to mescaline. According to Dawkins, this person told him that a bad trip is so awful that he wouldn't advise someone to try psychedelics. I touch upon this subject in my previous work, *The Mescaline Confession: Breaking through the Walls of Delusion*, a book that was endorsed by Graham Hancock, the aforementioned best-selling author, who has reviewed it and said that it is a "thought-provoking, heartfelt, informative and above all important book. Highly recommended to anyone who feels that things are not as they should be in the world today."

The person who introduced Aldous Huxley to mescaline was Dr. Humphry Osmond, an English psychiatrist with an impeccable bio. In fact, Dr. Osmond was the one who coined the term "psychedelic" at a psychiatrists' meeting at the New York Academy of Sciences in 1956. He explained that the word meant "mind manifesting" (from *psyche* [mind] and *delos* [manifest]) and called it "clear, euphonious and uncontaminated by other associations." He is also the author of the famous rhyme, "To fathom Hell or soar angelic, just take a pinch of psychedelic." He was known for his psychedelics research and achieved a 50% success rate in curing alcoholism using LSD. One of Osmond's patients during this time was William Griffith Wilson, who became a co-founder of Alcoholics Anonymous.

Dr. Osmond has dedicated his life to psychology and the study of schizophrenia, trying to understand its causes and find a cure. During this research he has also discovered the potential of psychedelics to generate profoundly mystical experiences, which led him to the famous encounter with Aldous Huxley that resulted in the eye-opening 1956 book, *The Doors of Perception*.

Later, Osmond became director of the Bureau of Research in Neurology and Psychiatry at the New Jersey Neuro-Psychiatric Institute in Princeton and a professor of psychology at the University of Alabama in Birmingham. Osmond co-wrote eleven books and was recognized for his contribution to the field of psychedelics and psychology.

He also participated in a Peyote ceremony hosted by members of the Red Pheasant tribe of Plains Indians. Osmond published his report in *Tomorrow*[21] magazine in 1961, including details of the ceremony, the environment in which it took place, the effects of the peyote, the courtesy of the participants, and his positive reflection of the whole event. Dr. Osmond's biography and professional life deserve our utmost respect. If anything, from this condensed bio, it is abundantly clear that Dr. Osmond was a big proponent of psychedelics, rather than one who would inspire Dawkins's negative, alarmist words.

Dawkins said that he was ready to try psychedelics only on his deathbed. A God debunker who refuses to expand his consciousness. It does not require courage to spend time in the library and write your own books with highly arrogant titles such as *The God Delusion* (2008) and his new book, *Outgrowing God* (2009) but it takes courage to set yourself on your psychedelic journey and discover the truth for yourself. At least, in this case, his words would have more weight and would be more objective if he had made this journey.

A bad trip is certainly one of the places where psychedelics can take you but definitely not the only one. Bad trips happen when a person approaches psychedelic experience in the wrong way, without guidance in a proper set and setting. This is what happened to Brian Greene, a theoretical physicist, as he described it on the Joe Rogan podcast[22].

The Cactus of Sanity

Brian never had had a psychedelic experience and decided to try it for the first time on the streets of Amsterdam after giving a lecture to the Queen of the Netherlands. This kind of experience would keep you from ever experimenting with psychedelics again. But whatever he smoked should not be blamed, but rather the poor set and setting. There is a proper way to take psychedelics that must be respected and followed, otherwise you set yourself up for trouble. But is it really different than driving a car without following road signs? If you don't stop at the red light and thus cause a deadly accident, who is to blame? Same with psychedelics.

When Rogan asked Dawkins whether or not consciousness was more than just a cognitive function of a brain, which he called a "reductionist approach," Dawkins objected by asking, "What's wrong with it?" Rogan changed the subject and missed the opportunity to challenge Dawkins. Personally, I like Joe Rogan. I think he is a sincere, funny and smart guy who is seeking answers and is using his platform to educate himself as much as entertain the audience. He seems to bring out what his guests wouldn't otherwise share in public, and, by doing that, he allows his viewer to hear what they actually think on different subjects. But if I were interviewing Dawkins then, I would have simply asked how mindless particles can create a mindful experience. If we all are quantum emptiness, how can there be Joe Rogan, Richard Dawkins or anyone else? I wonder what Richard Dawkins sees when he looks in a mirror — a quantum soup made of chemicals and electromagnetic signals bound together by the laws of physics? And what about love? Where does it come from? Is it not an emotional part of consciousness? Bricks don't love one another. Humans do.

In a TED Talk[23], psychiatrist Daniel Amen describes SPECT, a nuclear medicine study that looks at the blood flow and activity and how the brain works that studies 83,000 brain scans that done over 22 years in patients from 93 countries. He makes some interesting points about reversing brain damage by looking at the imaging and helping people with depression or self-destructive behavior. But after creating a largest brain imaging database in the world, they still learned nothing about consciousness. Amen does not even mention the word. The point is, no matter how many brains you scan, you won't see consciousness on the screen, and yet, here we are, aware, conscious and capable of seeing the Universe in a grain of sand, God in an atom and Eternity in a moment. Consciousness is what is actually looking at the images of the brain, trying to understand itself.

The Cactus of Sanity

To answer the question, "what is wrong with reductionism?" reductionism is the killer of magic, but only for the person who is reducing it. It is still present for others who perceive it as such. Reductionism kills everything that is beautiful, spiritual, poetic and loving. A reductionist scientist would look at the beauty of Nature and would see dead chemicals reflecting light, perceived by a retina that converts the light into neural signals that travel to the visual cortex and are decoded by the brain. He or she would deconstruct poetry into words, letters, sounds and frequencies, missing out on the message and feeling poetry conveys. They would reduce spirituality down to a shift of perception due a change in neural pathways and processes. Then they would demolish love and explain it as a chemical impulse and an increase and decrease of neurotransmitters in the brain.

Of course, for anyone who has ever loved, the notion that there is no such thing as love is just ludicrous. You know love by loving, not by measuring brain activity and its rising level of chemicals. Scientists believe that love consists of testosterone, estrogen, dopamine, oxytocin, serotonin and vasopressin, and they are not wrong. What they describe might be correct on the chemical level. But love is an experience that we know when we love. Who can measure my love for my children? Analytical thinking simply fails when it comes to conscious experiences, none of which can be measured or explained other than by offering cut and dried formulas. How dull must it be existing in a chemical cosmic soup without a sense of magic and love?

Spirituality is reverse engineering, an attempt to understand Divine principles by studying ourselves. That being said, the beauty of Nature provides healing and therapy, poetry conveys feelings, love creates emotions, spirituality leads to meaning. The chemical basis is present, but the experience is where the magic is. Reductionism takes away the magic of life, making existence boring and purely materialist. What if the body chemistry only responds to love rather than causing it, as science tends to see it?

I partly share Dawkins's position on religious indoctrination of children. But what does he have to offer instead? Consumerism, materialism and reductionist science? During one correspondence between Huxley and Osmond, Huxley said that "a contemporary education seemed typically to have the unintended consequence of constricting the minds of the educated — close the minds of students, that is, to inspiration and to many things other than material success and consumerism." I cannot agree with him more. This is the kind of education we currently have and it is the only alternative to religious indoctrination. Honestly, I don't know what's worse.

I find it fascinating that, in his podcast with Joe Rogan, Brian shares a conversation he had with Richard Dawkins, who revealed that he is scared of staying in haunted houses. Doesn't this mean that he believes in the supernatural? Do militant atheists believe in ghosts?

While being a critical thinker myself, I am against the toxic skepticism that I observe among the representatives of the atheist, scientific community. I would recommend that Richard Dawkins embrace a plant-based shamanic experience. I believe this would open him up to the aspects of reality hidden from a reductionist point of view. I would be happy to host him here in our retreat center in Peru where he would have nothing to worry about and be assured that his safety and sanity would remain intact.

CHAPTER 26

THE ELEPHANT IN THE ROOM

"Science without religion is lame. Religion without science is blind."

— Albert Einstein

Western monotheism has marginalized human experience by placing us in a category of sin, making us feel guilty for our birth and hopeless until forgiven through repentance. Such is Christianity, boiled down. Its counterpart, science, on the other hand, has gone further and made human life even less significant by stating that it, just like everything else in the Universe, is merely an accident that happened, from nothing and for no reason. Creationism and evolution are two competing narratives that both claim absolute knowledge of human origin. Both schools of thought, apart from being dubious, are denigrating and put humanity down. I have never found satisfaction in either.

Growing up, I had more questions than answers, as perhaps I do still today. My existential crisis began early on. At the age of five, I was already asking big questions. "Why do I exist? Who am I? Where did I come from and where will I go after?" I was asking myself and my parents. "Why does everything exist? It could be just nothing." I remember one night sitting at the table in my room, drawing, while imagining the world without me. "What would happen if I disappeared? Would this table, the bed, the closet, the room and the building disappear with me? If not, if all those things would be as they are, and it were just me who was gone, then what difference does my life make to the world, if it remains the same without me?" Neither my life nor my death would make any difference, only to me and my parents.

Where did these questions come from? How could they appear in my mind, growing up in a secular Jewish family in Soviet Union, an atheist, socialist state that was the only god that existed in the Universe? These questions rose within my psyche as if they were planted by someone. But by whom? It wasn't my parents; it certainly wasn't the kindergarten and later school teachers; and most certainly not the Communist party. This early wondering was not stimulated by outside influences. I always felt like I was born with it. It was so strong in me that as a kid I lost sleep thinking about these things. I had good, carrying and loving parents. They were from the working class, but we never were hungry. I had toys, bicycles and books. I had clothes and a warm place to live. I don't remember the word NO from my parents. They tried their best to satisfy my childish desires. Furthermore, it cannot be said that my spiritual inquiry was based in suffering or on some kind of lack. I loved my childhood. It was magical. I remember it vividly today. I just had all those questions in my head.

In my youth, I looked into physiology to find answers. I only found human anatomy, not mind, consciousness and soul. I have looked into astronomy. It explained only the celestial movements, not the Universe itself. I looked into poetry and literature, it brought me closer to myself but still there was a distance. By adolescence I had already experienced a midlife crisis. Spending time in the cemetery at nights while on MDMA, I was asking myself, what was the point of living? I began to think that my questions were in fact the only answers, and perhaps I had to find satisfaction in just asking questions.

My desire for spiritual knowledge was as strong as desire for love for a woman. It felt biological. My spiritual hunger was as strong as my desire for sex. I have no doubt that the origin of my spiritual impulse was inborn, not implanted by outside stimuli. It was fanned later, but the fire was burning from within and from the beginning. To deny its originality, for me, would be like denying the existence of my own parents. I always thought about life as a great mystery, and my time in it as a great chance to understand it. It wasn't until I stepped on a shamanic path that self-discovery began to unfold. My inner search has led me to shamanism and transformative, revealing and magical plant teachers in Peru, Mexico and North America. A talking silence became my teacher, in a language with which I was somehow familiar. Nothing had to be taken on faith; it was a matter of feeling. The Nature of mystical experience is private, it cannot be demonstrated or projected on a wall like a film. This is when I realized that it was naïve to think that one can receive awakening from a guru by a gesture, hug or smile. At best, one can be inspired; this is the purpose of a guru. Their light is theirs. In the rare, best case scenario, it can only show our own darkness and lead us out of it to our own light. From my own research and conversations with many people over the years, I've come to the conclusion that with rare notable exceptions you can follow a guru for your entire life, just to realize at the end that you were running in a spiritual hamster wheel. I have done my share of this circular walking.

Bertrand Russell said: "I do not pretend to be able to prove that there is no God. I equally cannot prove that Satan is a fiction. The Christian God may exist: so may the Gods of Olympus, or of ancient Egypt, or of Babylon. But no one of these hypotheses is more probable than any other: they lie outside the region of even probable knowledge, and therefore there is no reason to consider any of them."

How dull and hopeless! If I had followed this advice, I would never have found myself and my path in this life. People of all ages and all cultures have had their version of supernatural. The variation in names, customs and clothing did not diminish the presence of something higher in their lives. If you look at ancient Egypt, for example, esoteric mysticism is literally engraved in walls. If you look at ancient cultures of South America and Mexico, you find a similar thread woven in the fabric of ancient cultures, both literally and figuratively speaking. Although the names for the supernatural have differed among the cultures, the volume of testimonies left in all kinds of forms has reached our days, and the ancient whisper of mystery has reached our heart through them. Looking at the historic pattern of mysticism worldwide, where footprints have been left in monumental architecture, literature and living rituals, one realizes that one is witnessing a fact, not theory.

Sigmund Freud, the founder of psychoanalysis, said, "If one attempts to assign to religion its place in man's evolution, it seems not so much to be a lasting acquisition, as a parallel to the neurosis which the civilized individual must pass through on his way from childhood to maturity." Elsewhere, he also said that it is "well from time to time to be skeptical about one's skepticism." Apparently, Freud did not apply his axiom to himself. Otherwise, he would have deepened and broadened his research into antiquity and reached into the mystical roots of it, as Carl Jung, his closest student, did. How naïve is to think that psychology, which is a study of the mind, has the last word on the knowledge of the mind. Dismissive of spirit, Charles Darwin, Sigmund Freud, and the latter-day "saints" like Richard Dawkins, are all victims of their own unchecked intellect. Failing to see the mystery within themselves, they claim the mystery does not exist. The militant reductionist rationalism is just as boring as religious dogmatism. Both are the two sides of the same coin, and one rejects the validity of the other. The problem with rationalists' approach is that they believe that what cannot be measured does not exist. They see religion as a fabrication of the mind and not a response to something primordial, like an echo that you can hear in the mountains but fail to locate.

Although both Russell and Freud are respectable people that have made their contributions to human knowledge, they do not represent all of rationalism, *per se*. William James, Harvard professor of philosophy and psychology, had a different approach. He published his first contribution to the field of philosophy in 1880, the article, "The Sentiment of Rationality." One of its main points was that the sentiments are the mark of rationality. The professor of psychology even experimented with laughing gas, trying to understand the Nature of consciousness experientially. One can only imagine what his contribution to the fields of psychology, philosophy and literature would have been if he had been introduced to mescaline, or even better, to the Huachuma experience in its proper shamanic context. In any case, William James is an example of a rational man who has not lost touch with his intuitive part.

Science overlooks the religious impulse as a part of reason. The very attempt to understand our own existence is a part of our rational faculty. The spirit of inquiry is a part of human intelligence. Animals don't seem to be preoccupied with this matter. It's only humans, who are rational beings, who are tormented with the problem of existence. It follows logically that being rational implies an urge for self-discovery that is spiritual in essence. The ancestry of both science and religion is mysticism and magic, which is rejected by both as hateful children reject their parents. It appears that both religion and science feel comfortable to live under the delusion that they call "conclusion," while assuming their position as the final frontiers of knowledge.

Unfortunately, Freud did not make a distinction between the religious edifice of faith and religious experiences, which are not the same thing and can be experienced by people who have no religious background. The difference between religious thought and spiritual experience is great. One can lead to the other, but they are not the same. Religion, like any other object, casts a shadow. Just as the shadow you cast on a sunny day does not represent you, your intellect, your emotions, your set of values, your truths, your pain, your joy, your love and your hope, in the same way institutional religion does not represent religious experience that, in essence, is mystical. Religion's ideological buildings are higher than any skyscraper, and yet they do not reach the sky. They only block the light that an inquiring mind and intuitive soul can perceive. Both Russell and Freud are good examples. They could not see the hidden landscape behind the religious building; they could only see religious shadows cast on the human mind. Hence, they could not see the other side, just as with the moon. Modern day intellectuals are lacking this knowledge entirely, while being deluded by the authority of their own egos. Then, when confronted with spiritual subjects, they simply deny their existence.

To me, it is not much different than looking at the half moon in the night sky and deeming the other half non-existent because it cannot be seen. We know well that when the moon is full, we see it as it is; it's only a matter of light, or lack thereof, that makes the other half invisible. The moon is always only half for them. Lack of a spiritual sight is what makes the rationalist deny the spiritual reality. Their intellectual toolbox fails to measure the immeasurable, grasp the ungraspable, feel the infinite and eternal. What doesn't fit in their box that they call science, for them doesn't exist. Dogmatic scientific minds cannot lead us forward, just as orthodox faith cannot either. They have no idea how ridiculous they would appear to themselves in mystical ecstasy. Seeing themselves like monkeys wearing glasses, they would laugh and renounce their pride once and for all. Scientific arrogance is ridiculous to anyone who has seen the spiritual ground of reality even once, let alone for those who turned this ground into a farmland that grows consciousness like rice.

Science claims God is an illusion because it cannot measure God. Consciousness is the same; if you can't measure it, it doesn't exist. Consciousness is ungraspable by the intellect. What a tragic state of existence it is when the existence of existence itself is questioned! In the same way intuition, the "sixth sense" if you will, cannot be measured or its expression captured on a screen. It gets hijacked at an early age by organized religion, science, politics, and external authorities making a great effort to suppress our own. Power structures attempting to subvert consciousness by replacing it with all kinds of ideologies speaks only in favor of its existence. Ideologies are labyrinths of the mind that can only be escaped through a kind of rising above them, making you see them simply for what they are: theories, beliefs and assumptions. Plant-based shamanic experience lifts you above the cultural myths created by both religion and science.

Today, neuroscience still cannot explain the relationship between the mind and the brain, and still cannot explain the basic functions of how the mind works. How am I able to recall old memories in an instant, remembering being held by my father when I was three years old, as vividly now as 40 years ago? How do we imagine the future? How do we dream? None of it is actually explained, especially memory. How do we remember? We certainly know we do, but how? How does our basic brain function? We don't even understand how we can see with our eyes! We know the anatomy of the eye and know how photons are received by the retina and send signals to the visual cortex, but that only explains the mechanism of sight — not the actual experience of seeing. How arrogant is to assume knowledge of a higher-order experience such as spiritual sight, or even more, deny its very existence! If neuroscience cannot even explain the obvious, daily brain functions, how it can state with certainty that consciousness doesn't exist?

The same is true with physics, which claims that matter is primary and there is nothing beyond it. And yet physicists cannot fit their own theory of cosmic order into their theory of chaos. Electrons are spinning around the atomic nucleus in the same exact way as planets going around the star, and star clusters orbit around the center of a galaxy, all held together by the force of gravity. Huachuma showed me our galaxy once in a vision, like a Christmas tree seen from afar, full of shimmering lights constantly moving in some kind of order that was controlled by the force of gravity. Afterwards, when I opened my eyes, I called the force of gravity "the Divine Glue that holds the Universe together." But the force that holds stars and galaxies together is the same exact force that Newton discovered by watching an apple fall off a tree. The same force manifests itself on different scale.

Microcosms and macrocosms operate under the same principle; the same order on different scales cannot be a coincidence. Hermis Trismigistus, an ancient sage, spoke of a cosmic principle when he said "As above, so below." How can the chaotic Universe operate with precision and order? And in humans, how can unconscious particles create conscious experience? Our best ideas on both the human mind and the cosmos are just like those of children who speculate about where the sun goes after sunset.

But this rationalist's dryness is not a new phenomenon; it has ancient roots. Let's go back to Plato, nearly twenty-five hundred years ago. He too equated divine inspiration to madness:

"There is also a madness which is a divine gift, and the source of the chief blessing granted to men. For prophecy is a madness, and the prophetess at the Delphi and the priestesses at Dodona, when out of their senses, have conferred great benefits on Hellas, both in public and private life, but when in their sense few or none. And I might also tell you how the Sibyl and other inspired persons have given to many an intimation of the future which has saved them from falling. But it would be tedious to speak of what everyone knows."

"Then I knew that not by wisdom do poets write poetry, but by sort of genius and inspiration; they are like diviners or soothsayers who also say many fine things, but do not understand the meaning of them." (Plato's *Apology*)

To Plato, wisdom meant sanity and reason, but he equated inspiration to a form of madness. He dared to include poetry into the latter category while claiming that "poets often say fine things, the meaning of which they don't understand." How can a person who has no inspiration can judge those who have? By no means do I compare myself to the great minds produced over the course of human history, but even in my own humble experience, I don't see how it is possible to say or write something that I don't understand. And that's just me. According to his logic, Shakespeare wrote his sonnets without understanding their meaning. A flaw in thinking camouflaged as reason? Who am I to judge?

It is not widely known that Plato's teacher, the great Socrates, the father of rationalism, received his inspiration from the Oracle of Delphi. Trying to prove the Oracle wrong, Socrates became who he was to become. He was also guided by a voice, his Daemon: "You have often heard me speak of an oracle or sign which comes to me, and is the divinity which Meletus ridicules in the indictment. This sign I have had ever since I was a child. The sign is a voice which comes to me and always forbids me to do something which I am going to do, but never commands me to do anything, and this is what stands in the way of my being a politician." (Plato's *Apology*) Thus, Divine or inspired rationalism would be a better term to apply to Socrates, who not only became a sage but also a symbol of wisdom for eternity.

This very different state of affairs from modern day rationalism, which acquired new words but lost all wisdom. Modern science would dismiss Socrates's sources of inspiration. It may very well be that the academic consensus to remove revelation or insight, even the notions of them, from its curriculums altogether has less to do with disbelief and more with a desire to maintain the status quo by pushing reason to the top of the list of virtues scientists alone control. In a similar manner, religion maintains a narrative that its leaders control. The whole Inquisition was an attempt to sterilize mysticism, which could undermine the Catholic Church's monopoly over the Divine. Perhaps a revelation can be mad as madness can be revealing; nevertheless, to me it seems an exception to the rule, not the rule itself. The Catholic Church was a S.W.A.T. team designed to destroy all competition. An outbreak of mysticism would cast serious doubts that the Church is the only source of Divinity. Science took a different approach. It degraded mysticism to pathology. While fighting one another for human minds, science and religion came together against individual-based mysticism and intuitive insights.

The Cactus of Sanity

It is truly a pity that there is no modern day, well-known scholar who has anything thoughtful, let alone profound, to say about mystical experiences, prophetic visions and divine inspiration. Far worse, if we entrust modern day psychiatrists and psychologists with the interpretation of Divine inspiration, we will find our world to be hopeless and empty. They would rush to diagnose Socrates with schizophrenia at his first revelation of Daemon, his guiding inner voice. In ancient times, inspiration accounted for illuminated consciousness and prophetic vision. But modern science has lost its touch with the ancient Muse. Rationalism has lost its wisdom, and a genius has become insane. Following this logic, Shakespeare would be diagnosed with schizophrenia as well, and Hamlet would get him locked up in a psychiatric clinic. Upon admittance, he would meet Johann Wolfgang von Goethe, Dante Alighieri, William Blake and many others. Nevertheless, Shakespeare's "unbalanced" state of mind or hallucinations and hearing voices have made him and others immortal — the best textbooks for true students of the human mind. This is the type of psychology I like, psychology with spirit, literally and metaphorically. Intuitive insight is not a form of madness — perhaps the antidote to it, in fact. The limited understanding of the human mind leads to false conclusions, such as a human is a machine or a meat robot. If there is no soul, how could there be an inspiration? This, of course, doesn't mean that channeling Chewbacca from the sixth dimension it's somewhat spiritual, genuine or inspiring. Spirituality has little to do with appearance.

The problem with rationalism, or the analytical mind, is that it has presumed too much and declared itself a king of all kingdoms, even of those whose territories it didn't conquer or even explore. If psychology is the study of the mind, then its objective should be an exploration of the mind in all possible ways. This must include higher states of consciousness, which are accessible on demand. To claim knowledge of the human mind otherwise would be like describing an elephant by holding its tail. The parable of the Blind Men and an Elephant comes to mind. In it, a group of blind men who have never seen an elephant before, learn and conceptualize what the elephant is like by feeling a different part of the elephant's body, but only one part, such as the side or the tusk. They then describe the elephant based on their limited experience, and their descriptions of the elephant are different from each other. In some versions, they come to suspect that the other people are dishonest in their descriptions. This parable demonstrates human tendency to claim absolute truth based on limited experience and knowledge. Such is the claim of psychology, philosophy, science and religion, which all are touching a different part of an elephant that no one can see fully. The immense reality excluded from ordinary perception is not accounted for in the final conclusion described by science. It is as incomplete as a thesis on the anatomy of an elephant that consisted of a description of its leg. Nevertheless, a redacted version based on reduced observations has been presented as a complete account of life.

It seems as though the problem of science is that it has assumed authority over the world described by our five senses without asking if there is anything beyond it. Is the world described by the five senses all there is? Physics claims knowledge over matter while completely ignores metaphysical, realities that exist beyond our sense-perception. An argument against their existence is easily debunked by a plant-based shamanic experience, an experience that can be repeated and verified over and over again, which is in fact the main principle or technique that defines science. Leo Tolstoy said it best: "What we call science today is merely a haphazard collection of disconnected scraps of knowledge, most of them useless and many of which, instead of giving us absolute truth, provide the most bizarre delusions, presented as truth one day and refuted the next."

The positive side of science and the way it differs from any religious school of thought is that science is the only one that has the courage to prove itself wrong. One scientist forms a hypothesis just for another to do further research and prove it wrong. It is trial and error, which is fluid and transparent like water. It is more honest, and honesty leads to truth. Too often, its colleagues on the other side never do that. No priest questions his revered texts and handed-down narratives. It's all static, it never changes. This is its weakness. It is solidified into a dogma and sanctified as holy. Theistic religion has no appeal to a rational mind, let alone to a mind that psychedelic experience has expanded. The inconsistencies that are observed in life, such as wars, diseases, hunger and suffering, cause one to question the existence of a benevolent, compassionate God. How can he allow all this to happen in his own backyard, to his own children? Such inconsistencies are the result of dogmatism and misunderstanding. Scientists, on the other hand refuses to accept the possibility of extra sensory perception, calling it delusional and hallucinatory. It would be very easy to prove them wrong if they were willing to challenge their narrative. What would be hard, however, is for scientists to accept a humiliating experience that would force them to rethink and revise their concepts, assumptions, theories and what they call "facts".

Lord Kelvin, the prominent 19th century Irish scientist, expressed one of the most negative views towards psychic phenomena: "Clairvoyance and the like were the result of bad observation chiefly, somewhat mixed up with the effects of willful imposture, acting on an innocent trusting mind that wretched superstition of animal magnetism and table and spiritualism and mesmerism and clairvoyance of which we have heard so much." This is true, to a point. When we speak about the charlatan medium who sells his predictions on the street, or a healer who snaps his fingers in front of a patient with some kind of a cartoonish abracadabra spell, then Lord Kelvin's words resonate with truth. However, to include all spiritual masters in this category would be a rather mindless generalization. His words would include the Oracle of Delphi, the visionaries and prophets of antiquities, the mystics and sages of all times, who all possessed spiritual and psychic faculties that, according to Lord Kelvin, would be nothing more than delusions and frauds.

Western science is purely materialistic, and its reductionist approach prevents researchers from accessing the metaphysical realm. There is simply no science of higher consciousness in the Western school of thought. Psychology, anthropology, philosophy and religion all are dealing with the expression, customs, ideas and beliefs; they study the form but not the cause. There is a way of direct perception that bypasses both beliefs and intellect — a call that religion is at least trying to answer, but science can't even hear. Intuition is a faculty superior to reason that allows us to see into places invisible to scientific and religious dogmas. Spiritual knowledge or a higher level of consciousness is received not with faith or reason but through contemplation and intuition. It's an ability to perceive beyond words and concepts — a sixth sense, or super-sense, or higher sense. It cannot be taught in a class.

Children feel with intuition. They are much closer to the truth than any academic. They feel and know their existence, they don't think about it. Intuition is our innate compass that gets mistuned as we grow up, and in most cases it becomes completely silent and unheard of underneath the constant mind chattering. This is our human tragedy. We are born all right, but then we get corrupted by the cultural influences that feast like vultures on our innocence until we grow dull. This is why, as a parent, it is extremely important to help your children to maintain that sense of magical connection with themselves and the world they live in during adolescence. As their personality forms, their spirit of wonder, intuition and a sense of miraculousness must remain intact.

The more I think about it, the more I become convinced that the higher consciousness that has been observed in a small portion of humanity throughout history — in mystics, prophets and sages — was a demonstration of and possible prelude to an evolutionary stage in which all humanity reaches this state of mystical consciousness and thus completes a very long evolutionary cycle. This state of Oneness would be a final revelation to humanity, in which the revealer and the revealed become one. Physics states that, at a fundamental level of matter, an observed phenomenon cannot be separated from the observer. In the same way in a mystical experience, an observed Godhood is inseparable from the observer. This realm that has been entirely dismissed by science is, perhaps, the ultimate science. But how can there be a study of cosmic consciousness if rationalists deny consciousness exists? You've got to start somewhere.

The degree of perception that is accessible to the higher states of consciousness is much greater than the one experienced by the five senses. The extra sensory perception that becomes abundantly active with the help of plant teachers such as Ayahuasca, Huachuma and Peyote is the last nail in the coffin of skepticism, non-Divine rationalism and analytical thinking. It simply reveals the limitations of ordinary perception, the very foundation of modern science. Thus, the academic, reductionist view that assumed absolute authority over knowledge cannot penetrate through the veil of mystery, which is as thin and transparent as spider's web. The 500 years of war between religion and science has led to science becoming that which it was fighting against, a dogmatic institution. And in the same exact way that religion held authority over divine matters, science championed denialism without proof. If religion has a God figure somewhere in the sky, science replaces God with intellect — an intellect that just fairly recently shed the old skin of a brute.

Reason is a part of a personality, it's the ego. Its role is transitional, to preserve the species from self-destruction while it is evolving into higher consciousness. Reason, like money, is only a means to an end, not the end itself. The error of religion, to exclude reason from its narrative, is just as limiting a factor as for science to deny religious sentiment altogether. The reason for the conflict of opinions between religion and science is that both are using different tools to understand the same phenomena and both assume that their tools are final. Neither of them, however, understand that all of their tools are useful only to a point. Either a belief or measurement will get you only so far.

Science forgot something that religion remembers. The problem with religion is that its memory has lost vividness and become rigid. It has lost the ability to reproduce religious experience. It became a painting on a wall in a house of worship. Karl Marx said, "Religion is a sigh of the oppressed creature, the heart of a heartless world and the soul of soulless conditions. It is the opium of the people." I could argue with Marx, from personal experience, that using opium in my youth wasn't the same as religion, even in its most dogmatic form. Religion is a map, opium is oblivion. The map is lacking an address, yet still it shows a general landscape that must be explored individually.

Neither religion nor science have emphasized the importance of the visionary experiences that have preceded both. Life is made of dreams, both godly and human. Ancient religious literature is full of such encounters, and these are widely known. However, the visionary experiences that preceded science have been emphasized to a lesser extent, perhaps with the intent to bury it, for it defeats the materialist Nature of science itself. But as it is very difficult for a mammal to escape a sharp sight of a hunting hawk, it is difficult for significant events to escape the mind of a reader. Such a significant event happened on November 10, 1619 when a young philosopher, Rene Descartes, had a series of three dreams in which he was taught scientific methods by an Angel of Truth, an event that not only has shaped his own life but also paved the way of science forward by providing him with scientific methods. This Angel of Truth revealed a secret, like a flash of lighting, which lay the foundation of a new method of understanding a "new marvelous science." Inspired and taught by an Angel, Descartes began a treatise called "Rules for the Direction of the Mind," whose objective was to describe the workings of the mind. His later, famous "Discourse on Method," taken as a founding document of modern philosophy, was, too, rooted in Angelic inspiration. Interestingly, both Descartes and his future followers all leave this pivotal fact out of his biography, thanks to which Descartes became a father figure of modern science.

Another, more recent example for an inspired science is demonstrated in Kukule's dream. A renowned German chemist of the 19th century, Friedrich August Kekulé, discovered the ring shape of the benzene molecule after having a day-dream of a snake seizing its own tail. The first known representation of this symbol, the ouroboros, is depicted in the shrine enclosing the sarcophagus of Tutankhamun. Thus, a vision of an ancient alchemical symbol of eternal rebirth became a part of modern chemistry without much acknowledgment and recognition.

The famous chemist Dmitri Mendeleev was obsessed with finding a logical way to organize the chemical elements. He could not do it with his waking consciousness. Intuitively feeling that he was about to make a significant discovery, he wrote elements' names on cards and fell asleep at his desk. Upon awakening from sleep, the riddle was solved. He later wrote: "In a dream I saw a table where all the elements fell into place as required. When I woke up, I immediately wrote it down on a piece of paper."

Louis Agassiz was the world's foremost expert on fish species, both current and extinct. Once, after two weeks of intense striving, he still could not reconstruct the structure of an ancient fish. Exhausted, he gave up and tried to dismiss it from his mind. For three consecutive nights, he kept seeing the full image of the fish but could not recall it in the morning. On the third night he placed a pencil and paper beside his bed before going to sleep. Towards morning the fish reappeared in his dream, with such distinctness that he had no longer any doubt as to its zoological affinity. Still half dreaming, in the darkness of the night, he followed his nightly vision with a pen on paper.

Otto Loewi, a German-born pharmacologist and psychobiologist who discovered the role of acetylcholine as an endogenous neurotransmitter and was awarded the Nobel Prize in Physiology or Medicine in 1936, was trying to find a way to prove that nerve signals were transmitted using chemical instructions. In 1920 Loewi had a dream about the problem. He woke excitedly during the night and wrote down what he saw in a dream. The problem was solved.

Srinivasa Ramanujan, a mathematical genius who, by 32, produced nearly 4,000 proofs, identities, conjectures and equations in pure mathematics. Elliptic functions and number theory are just a few of his contributions that continue to inspire mathematicians today. Ramanujan said that the Hindu goddess Namagiri would appear in his dreams teaching him math, which he would write down when he woke up in the morning. He described one of his dreams as follows: "There was a red screen formed by flowing blood, as it were. I was observing it. Suddenly a hand began to write on the screen. I became all attention. That hand wrote a number of elliptic integrals. They stuck to my mind. As soon as I woke up, I committed them to writing."

Alfred Russel Wallace, Darwin's contemporary, a traveler and a researcher, was struggling with the question of the birth of new species. In 1858, he had a delirious dream, caused by a tropical fever. When the fever had gone, he realized that he discovered the theory of evolution by natural selection.

Niels Bohr, the father of quantum mechanics discovered the structure of the atom in a dream. Struggling with his configurations, one night he went to sleep and began dreaming about atoms. He saw the nucleus of the atom, with electrons spinning around it, much as planets spin around their sun. After further research, his night vision proved to be correct. Bohr was later awarded the Nobel Prize for Physics as a result of this leap in creative thinking while asleep.

Albert Einstein, as it happens, came to the extraordinary scientific achievement of discovering the principle of relativity after having a vivid dream in which he was sledding down a steep mountainside with ever increasing speed, until he reached the speed of light. At this moment, the stars in his dream changed their appearance in relation to him. He awoke and meditated on this idea, soon formulating what would become one of the most famous scientific theories in history.

Frederick Banting, after the death of his mother from diabetes, was motivated to find a cure. Following a sequence of dreams, he came up with a treatment using insulin injections that, though not a true cure, could at least significantly extend the lifespan of sufferers. The discovery won him the Nobel Prize in Medicine at just 32 years old.

There are many more examples of writers, artists and others who dream songs, poems and books that later were manifested into pieces of art. Mary Shelley conceived *Frankenstein*, the world's first sci-fi novel, in a vivid dream: "I saw the pale student of unhallowed arts kneeling beside the thing he had put together. I saw the hideous phantasm of a man stretched out, and then, on the working of some powerful engine, show signs of life, and stir with an uneasy, half vital motion. Frightful must it be; for supremely frightful would be the effect of any human endeavor to mock the stupendous mechanism of the Creator of the world."

Paul McCartney composed the entire melody for the hit acoustic song "Yesterday" in a dream. He later wrote: "For about a month I went round to people in the music business and asked them whether they had ever heard it before.

The Cactus of Sanity

Eventually it became like handing something in to the police. I thought if no-one claimed it after a few weeks then I could have it."

Robert Louis Stevenson dreamed of the story of his thriller fiction novel, *The Strange Case of Dr. Jekyll and Mr. Hyde*. "For two days I went about racking my brains for a plot of any sort; and on the second night I dreamed the scene at the window, and a scene afterward split in two, in which Hyde, pursued for some crime, took the powder and underwent the change in the presence of his pursuers."

Giuseppe Tartini is an Italian composer and violinist best known for his Devil's Trill Sonata, which he composed after the Devil appeared in his dream, delivering an intense violin performance. Tartini recounted his vision to French writer Jérôme Lalande, who included the story in his travel memoir *Voyage d'un François en Italie, fait dans les années 1765 & 1766*:

"Tartini dreamed one night, in 1713, that he had made a compact with the Devil, who promised him to be at his service on all occasions; and during this vision everything succeeded according to his mind. In short, he imagined he gave the Devil his violin, in order to discover what kind of musician he was; when to his great astonishment, he heard him play a solo so singularly beautiful and executed with such superior taste and precision, that it surpassed all he has ever heard or conceived in his life. So great was his surprise and so exquisite his delight upon this occasion that it deprived him of the power of breathing.... He awoke with the violence of his sensation and instantly seized his fiddle in hopes of expressing what he had just heard, but in vain; he, however, then composed a piece, which is perhaps the best of all his works (he called it the 'Devil's Sonata') but it was so inferior to what his sleep had produced that he declared he should have broken his instrument and abandoned music forever, if he could have subsisted by any other means."

At last but not the least, I myself can attest to this dream learning. In my first book, I shared a story about coming back from Peru and having a dream in which I was taught how to make Huachuma medicine. Back then I still was living in California and only traveled to Peru periodically to work with Huachuma cactus. In this dream, I was preparing Huachuma. When I woke up, I went and cut one of the cacti that had been growing in my garden for years but had never been cut before. I was waiting for a sign that came in a dream with an instruction. Also, as I began writing books after moving to Peru, on countless nights I dreamed entire passages during the night. Being too lazy to wake up and thinking that there was no way I could forget the words in the morning, I did not write them down. But I could not recall anything the next day. I started to keep pen and paper at night and forced myself to wake up to write things down. My second book, *The Mescaline Confession*, started at about 3:00 AM one night when I woke up and began writing.

The point I'm trying to get across is that reason is just a tool, a useful tool to go by in worldly affairs but limited in application to Divine matters. We can call it the unconscious mind, the Other, an inspiration, a sign, a Daemon voice, or any other name. There is something beyond what a rational mind can grasp that keeps guiding and inspiring many people through history, something that science calls delusional, delirious and hallucinatory, while religion refers to it as demonic. We can debate its origin, whether it is our unconscious mind or an outside force, but the facts of its existence are, to me, doubtless and beyond all debate. My whole life is a movement between the two, the rational and the elusive, the awake and the lucid. Being saved many times from serious troubles in life, I was put back on the path by an invisible hand sensible only to intuition. I know for a fact that there is more to us than flesh and bones. We are quarter animal, quarter human, quarter spirit and quarter God. We are all in one and one in all. Our Divine heritage is forgotten to our mind, but it is present in our souls. This part needs awakening. None of this dwells in a realm of reason, which is a boat to get us across the river on our way to the ocean. When we get to the ocean, we need a bigger boat, a ship of consciousness to sail through the Universe.

But what is even more interesting is the fact that we can influence that other side of us, the lucid, the dreamy, the intuitive and the sensitive. We don't have to rely on chance and hope that a Muse will spot us down here among nearly 8 billion people and guide us through the madness of the modern world. We can play an active role in attracting the force by simply opening up to it via the plant teachers. This is a direct way out of the labyrinths of the mind, a vertical ascension into the intuitive knowing. This is what I was thinking — or dreaming — at a very ancient cave in Bolivia that I once visited to explore prehistoric rock art. My companions and I did a ceremony right in front of the wall painting and stayed there all day in contemplation.

The Cactus of Sanity

While contemplating the wall paintings, I thought, just 40,000 years or so ago, our human ancestors were just learning their ways to be human. They were the founders of human consciousness. What is 40,000 years in a scheme of 4.5 billion, which is thought to be the age of the Earth? It's just a moment. And here we are ready to destroy the planet with nuclear bombs to settle ideological disputes. Although we are young and promising species, we are extremely dangerous. We need guidance from Nature, not rhetoric from politicians. We need plant teachers, not nuclear plants. We need a genuine connection with ourselves and other human beings, not Facebook friends.

The Cactus of Sanity

Thinking about all this, I drifted away to a far distant past where there was no life yet. The earth had just only cooled off and was setting the stage for life. I saw nothing there but a purpose. I inquired into it more and was shown that life on Earth was that purpose. The raw mass of cooling Earth was an embryo, and the yet to be formed organic life on its surface was its soul. Life, as I saw it, was not an accident but a certainty, in the same way as a fully formed human being is a certainty that is formed in an embryo. Earth was the body, the mother's womb; the sun was the father; and we, I thought, are the Earth's children in a literal sense. No wonder why the ancient cultures of Peru related to Earth as mother and the sun as the father. They knew this too. It may sound primitive to a Western rationalist, but it is logically sound and scientifically provable. There could be no life on Earth without the sun that gives life. And there could be no life without the Earth that is the egg to be fertilized by the sunlight.

I thought about life on other Earth-like planets, and it was logical to assume that life on them would be just as certain as it is on our planet, given that all conditions are met. The planet must be fully formed to host life, as an egg must be fertile. I saw infinite possibilities for life in the Universe and this was its purpose: to procreate itself further, to expand into the everywhere and the always, the divine propagation of life and light. I thought about the Big Bang that is considered to be the beginning of time and the Universe. I saw it as a cosmic orgasm that fertilized the egg of the newly born Universe, like a child born from a mother. This led to thinking that there could be more Universes before ours, one giving birth to another, and so it goes forever, like the ouroboros on a gigantic cosmic scale, the divine principle of life and death. I thought about God. It was a purpose. Life's purpose was God's will. God was a Universal force. I mentally asked a question: Who were we in God's purpose? The answer was in the question. We were God's purpose. We were the expected children. As parents, we don't know how our children will look before they are born, but we anticipate it with amusement.

In the same way God, or the Universe, anticipates new consciousness to emerge from matter. Human consciousness has been anticipated; it wasn't an accident that happened without a reason. And plant teachers are the mother's breast milk that birthed it in a brute: the human race, which now has a huge responsibility for. We were brought into being by incredible circumstances with love, the same force that has fertilized the planet, the same force that lit the sun, the same force that gave birth to the Universe. The parental love given to children on a humongous cosmic scale is the same love we feel in our hearts toward our children, our loved ones, animals and life in general. Love is self-rewarding. Love, I thought, does not expect its progeny to be what it wants it to be but anticipates with wonder, like a parent, which I can attest to from experience. I want to give my children the opportunity to grow and choose what they want to be doing in life, not what I want them to do. Out of love, I respect their freedom. It felt to me it was the same case with divine love for humanity and life in general. It provides the necessary conditions that are required in order to create life, but it lets it be what it chooses to be. It explains the concept of free will and the Divine mind's non-interference policy.

I felt that if I could have dwelt on this vision for a bit longer, I could have understood the infinite, but I was distracted by a loud sound of bird, dissipating the intense vision among the Bolivian chaparral. I could not return to it, as one cannot return to a dream when briefly awakens from it. One only retains the memory of it but not the dream itself. Waking up from this lucid dream, the thought occurred to me that a cave is an ear of a mountain, to which we can put our own ears to hear ancient stories. Apart from minerals and rocks, mountains are also made of memories.

The Cactus of Sanity

If science is an exploration of Nature, shamanism is an exploration of Nature's experience, the study of metaphysics in physics. Sacred plants are physical, but their dimensions are metaphysical.

When I think about the emergence of human consciousness, I think of a miracle not lesser than life itself. Animals that began to think and speak — something amazing that we take for granted, or much worse, deny even exists. It is rather baffling that science does not recognize its own theory of evolution being equally miraculous as the theory of Creation. And just as the story of God's creation of Adam from dust sounds impossible to a rational mind, so does the process of an ape transforming into Socrates, Shakespeare, Vivaldi,

Leonardo da Vinci, Michelangelo, and others. While we would call it a miracle if it happened overnight, we fail to see this miracle manifesting during a longer period of time. What an incredibly intelligent force that has taken an animal and transformed it into a rational human being, capable of soul-searching contemplation and timeless art that continues to inspire future generations! Regardless what theory you believe in, both are equally fantastic. Human origin aside, consciousness is a miracle within a miracle that no one seems to understand, but everyone is arguing about. Instead, it might be useful to contemplate the role of sacred plants in human evolution. Perhaps these are our spiritual parents whom we were seeking in the sky. My search for Paradise was over the day I had my first Huachuma experience.

Awakening in this dream is the purpose of our existence, awakening to this miracle of life and seeing it like a child, full of wonder. Awakening can be likened to reverse engineering. It's a process by which our ego is deconstructed to its primal stage of existence, decrystallization into its original form. Crystals form in Nature when liquid hardens. Our ego is that hardened crystal that needs to be melted down into the primordial magma of being. The fabric of consciousness is fluid like water, bright like sunlight and light like air and yet

The Cactus of Sanity

solid as a rock, mysterious as the night sky and persistent as the seasons.

Everything has finally fallen into place, and all my past life events are full of meaning, but only after I made peace and embraced them rather than running away from them. My past and I became friends again. Accepting it has changed the course of my life. A strong desire to share this incredible world of beauty with others has become my work and livelihood. From all that I have experienced and contemplated in my life, I find the most viable approach to spiritual reality is through plant teachers. It is crucial to preserve shamanic knowledge for future generations. Without it, the world will sink into the perpetual chaos of words and concepts.

I feel like a quote from Ralph Waldo Emerson would be the best way to complete this book.

"This is my wish for you: Comfort on difficult days, smiles when sadness intrudes, rainbows to follow the clouds, laughter to kiss your lips, sunsets to warm your heart, hugs when spirits sag, beauty for your eyes to see, friendships to brighten your being, faith so that you can believe, confidence for when you doubt, courage to know yourself, patience to accept the truth, Love to complete your life."

EPILOGUE

CUSCO, WHERE ANCIENT HISTORY KEEPS COMING BACK WITH MORE

"The important thing is not to stop questioning. Curiosity has its own reason for existing. One cannot help but be in awe when he contemplates the mysteries of eternity, of life, of the marvelous structure of reality. It is enough if one tries merely to comprehend a little of this mystery every day. Never lose a holy curiosity."

— Albert Einstein

Running some errands in Cusco one day, I stumbled upon an excited crowd of people standing around the fenced area at the top of Avenida El Sol, a central street in Cusco. I didn't waste time thinking that the reason for their excitement was Peruvian workers jackhammering the colonial road. Anticipation of an archeological discovery began to settle in. Getting closer, my premonition was confirmed.

The Cactus of Sanity

Between many people staring at the newly uncovered site, I saw an archeological complex appearing from the ground. It took a minute to make a new friend: the archeologist in charge. Sharing with her my interest in the subject, she gave me permission to actually get down into the site for a visual inspection. It was quite sobering to find myself in the middle of central Cusco, just a few feet below the familiar road, walked on by millions of tourists each year. It is highly likely that, if you have visited Cusco, you walked this road yourself, knowing nothing about what's been hiding below, frozen in time. The street under which the complex was found is called Calle Mantas, which connects Avenida El Sol and the Plaza de Armas, the main square in what is today called the historical center of Cusco. Inspecting the site closely, however, I was not impressed. I would hardly call it a major archeological discovery, much less a mind-boggling piece of ancient architecture that would make one wonder about who built it and how, when and why? It was rather a typical Inca construction with stairways and walls, which can be seen in many areas in the Cusco region.

The Cactus of Sanity

Struggling with disappointment, I began to see another meaning, more subtle and significant than the site itself. It was the contrast between the ancient world and ours, now overlapping one another in real time. It was surreal to see how the gap of 500 years had now been breached by a minor dig that wasn't even meant to make history.

The Cactus of Sanity

Standing in the middle of it while surrounded by the noise of busy streets, I thought about how much more knowledge is hiding underground, making history by appearing to us in pieces, which are glued together with theories rather than welded with facts. This particular site didn't seem to bear any great significance other than it served as a vivid example of the cultural layers being swept underground by time.

How much more is yet to be uncovered, and yet, we assume with certainty that we know all about our history, I thought, between the chorus of cameras and chats. Almost hysterically, I began to take pictures, thinking about the limited time I had before being asked to leave. Before I was done, though, I had a chance to speak with the archeologist again to express my concern about this site being paved over as originally planned. The reconstruction of the roads in central Cusco was a project intended to replace colonial bricks with new pavement. In fact, walking up the Avenida El Sol that morning before arriving at the newly discovered Inca ruins on the top, I thought about the loss of charm the streets have suffered due to the current renovation project.

I didn't spare words in order to convey the importance of preserving this site and leaving it open so it can serve as a reminder of the Spanish conquest of Peru for future generations. The new road didn't matter, I said to the archeologist. People don't come to Peru to see paved roads, they have better ones at home. They do, however, come because they hear the ancient voices echoing through silent ruins, calling them to ponder our human past. The archeologist agreed with me and added that this, unfortunately, wasn't her decision.

Feeling some sadness, I crossed the road to the main square and sat on a bench to ponder it, while watching the ever-growing crowd around the site. Though I took pictures, I realized that I would never be able to transmit the atmosphere of that experience. In my books I have written about the brutality of the Spanish conquest and its implications for the native culture. But what I felt standing at the site and looking at the proudly rising Cathedrals built on the top of the Incan city, signifying triumph, could not be printed on paper or shared in words. It was a feeling present in the hearts of conquered people centuries ago.

Sitting on the bench, I thought about human vices, which are everywhere and always the same. How is our world today different from the world we are seeing underground? The striking progress I can see is in the tools and means of conquest and control, not in morals. We, in fact, are still barbaric people who are in urgent need of renaissance. What will it take to learn from the past and see that we repeating the same mistakes today? Is there any safety, peace and happiness to be found in a world run by religious fanaticism, political corruption and corporate greed? This took me deep into the debris of the medieval ages and even further into the human soul until the cool Cusco evening breeze finally brought me back.

Going home I thought about all those people who visit Peru each year in search of answers, some of them perhaps being unaware of their inner quest. Looking at their faces at the ancient sites and other places, I often see a genuine search for something real, something on the unconscious level they know exists. In this, I see a hope for the preservation of antiquity that continues to be fed with human wonder.

However, while all that is interesting, the real treasure of Peru is not found below the ground or built above it, but is growing in the land. Huachuma is the real gold, a great revealer and the best kept secret of the ancient Peru. Today, however, the world we live in requires healing. The way shamanic experience has become accessible in the last decade signifies the great need for plant medicine shamanism. Direct spiritual experience is the answer to many questions.

"Entheogens" is a term often used to describe psychoactive plants that have a history of being used for healing in various indigenous cultures. "Entheo" means "God within" and "gen" means "origin" or "generator": the generators of God within, a term familiar to researchers and practitioners. Entheo-archeology is the practice of performing Huachuma ceremonies at ancient archeological sites with the intent to connect to and feel the energy of these places. It is not an academic discipline. It is something I learned from my first teacher, Don Howard Lawler, with whom I traveled on a numerous occasions to Chavin de Huantar in Ancash, Peru, to the pyramids of Moche and Lambayaqe cultures, where we held Huachuma ceremonies to connect to the ancient cultures. We used Huachuma cactus instead of a trowel and a hand brush to uncover ancient history.

The human element combined with the beauty of Nature creates a very special experience. Different places have different energies, all unique in their own right. My most amazing and profound experience of it was when I came first to Peru in 2005. Although the term was new to me, the practice wasn't. Since I was 18 years old, when I took MDMA for the first time, exploring ancient sites and connecting to them in an altered state of consciousness that allows for direct perception had been my dream. I thought about going to Egypt and taking it there, in front of the Great Sphinx and the pyramids, to sit in silence and contemplate their ancient secrets. But I went without any psychoactive equipment, so it didn't happen. If I got caught with drugs, I would wind up in an Egyptian jail and never get out. It still was amazing to walk on the Giza plateau and see it all, even if through ordinary consciousness.

But when, years later, I met Don Howard in Peru and did Huachuma ceremonies at various ancient sites, I knew I was living a dream. A whole new dimension of Huachuma medicine opened up to me. At such places the focus of the work shifts from therapeutic to purely mystical and magical. Huachuma is the key to the hidden energy fields that are present in each place, either man-made or natural. Every place has its own energetic signature that you can read by contemplation. In Peru, every mountain is a different being who has a name. It might sound superstitious at first, but when I take you around, you will feel it yourself.

The Cusco region, which includes the Sacred Valley and Machu Picchu, is an archeological treasure island for those fascinated with the ancient cultures of Peru. Nearly four million people travel to Peru annually to enjoy the sightseeing. Many places will take your breath away: high altitude lakes with their stunning beauty and serene aura; ancient sites with buildings, caves, portals, and carvings in the rocks. But when we do our ceremonies, we do them privately, removed from other people. In order to hear an ancient echo in stones, one's mind must be quiet.

The Cactus of Sanity

Everything feels different when you find yourself looking at the world from high mountain peaks, surrounded by ancient ruins, sitting quietly on the ground and contemplating the natural beauty around you. Up here, where you can touch the clouds with your breath, life feels different. It makes you see yourself in a different light and with great clarity, as a masterpiece that completes itself in love. It truly is an experience outside of time that can transform your life. You can sense the ancient spirits in the wind.

Emerson, in his essay, "Nature," wrote:

"The incommunicable trees begin to persuade us to live with them, and quit our life of solemn trifles. Here no history, or church, or state, is interpolated on the divine sky and the immortal year. How easily we might walk onward into opening landscape, absorbed by new pictures, and by thoughts fast succeeding each other, until by degrees the recollection of home was crowded out of the mind, all memory obliterated by the tyranny of the present, and we were led in triumph by Nature.

These enchantments are medicinal, they sober and heal us. These are plain pleasures, kindly and native to us. We come to our own, and make friends with matter, which the ambitious chatter of the schools would persuade us to despise. We never can part with it; the mind loves its old home: as water to our thirst, so is the rock, the ground, to our eyes, and hands, and feet. It is firm water, it is cold flame; what health, what affinity! Ever an old friend, ever like a dear friend and brother, when we chat effectively with strangers, comes in this honest face, and takes a grave liberty with us, and shames us out of our nonsense."

Here in the Sacred Valley, this feeling is magnified to the maximum. You feel a transmission of energy between the ancient world, our world and the future generations. You are experiencing life from a perspective of thousands of years. From this state of consciousness, an ancient Egypt becomes within your reach, as does ancient Mexico or any other site on Earth. You feel the people who built them. You understand the expression of their divine connection. These places of worship become yours from a great distance. And yours become theirs. You feel united with the current of human knowledge and consciousness that has stretched through thousands of years. Millennia become sensible and graspable with your mind. You can actually feel a timescale of 10,000 years or more.

I remember visiting Chavin de Huantar for the first time with Don Howard. When we entered the labyrinths, the

The Cactus of Sanity

initiation chambers, and sat in silence at the peak of Huachuma experience, I began to feel like what was happening 3,000 years ago in this place was actually happening now, as though I was present at a Huachuma ceremony conducted by Chavin shamans. Mentally I knew that three millennia had passed, but experientially, it felt different. 3000 years had somehow vanished; there was no time between us. Time, I thought, was elusive and Huachuma collapses it into non-being. It was there and at the same time it wasn't.

Mother Nature is open for collaboration; she is giving us her hands in the form of plant teachers. And her hands are firm, like the hand of God depicted in Michelangelo's painting, "The Creation of Adam," a fresco that forms part of the Sistine Chapel's ceiling. It depicts the Biblical narrative in which God gives life to Adam. As an artist, Michelangelo expressed his own understanding in his work. Like all of us, he was seeking his answers. Whatever meaning he placed in it was his and is open for interpretation. But the great task in life is not to decode other people's work. Although this might be helpful and entertaining, the real task is to find your own meaning, form your own understanding and learn from direct experience. Reclaiming your mind from ideologies and belief systems is not taught in schools, universities, churches, synagogues, ashrams or monasteries. In fact, these are the promoters of myths. Psychedelic education provides an insight into what's actually real and all that has been taken away from us by these institutions. The bottom line is, it tells you that your life matters and you are your own teacher. This is the essence of shamanic experience.

Every creature wants to live. Every creature intrinsically carries this principle. We see its highest manifestation in a lonely stalk of grass breaking through concrete and reaching out to the light. So courageous, so powerful, so life affirming. The story of Creation would serve a greater good if it were depicted as the story of connection between a human being and nature. The distance between humanity and God in this painting is not great as religious and spiritual leaders tell us. Their two fingers are almost touching, a gap that can be easily bridged by a direct spiritual experience. If I were the author of this painting, I would add a Huachuma cactus somewhere in it, as a hint.

The Cactus of Sanity

The question remains, will we respond to her friendly gesture or turn our backs on her on our way to oblivion? We must replace our lethargy with liturgy to bridge that short distance to the Divine. You don't have to worship in public. Your communion with the Great Spirit of Life is internal and can be practiced in the silence of your own heart. A silent prayer made with love has a greater range. When you take Huachuma, all you see around, including yourself, is a work of art, Divine art, which completes itself in love. Life becomes so much easier and joyful when we simply embrace ourselves and tune our spirit to the healing beauty of Nature.

A cactus grows in the wild, but it is the raw material. Medicine is what we make of it. It is our version of the alchemical process of turning lead into gold. Lead is the plant material; gold is a profound spiritual experience. Ten people could use the same cactus, and there would be ten different versions and ten different experiences only slightly resembling one another. Medicine is the result, a mirror that reflects the person who is making it. It is a fusion of love, dedication, knowledge and experience with the cactus.

Making medicine is an ancient art that is not to be taken lightly. Knowing how to cut the cactus and dry or boil it and then thinking that you know it all, is like looking at an airplane in the sky and thinking you can fly it. As the cactus can be seen as liquid sun, so can the medicine man or woman absorb the medicine within themselves and become it. How can you decide whom to work with? Simply follow your feeling about the person who serves the medicine. In the exact same way you go out for a date, you choose a medicine person to take it with. Resonance is really the key, as with everything else in life. You have to like the person to be with a person.

In the same way as no one else can tell you what love is, no one can tell you what the meaning of life is. It is something

The Cactus of Sanity

that we all must find for ourselves. My experience and understanding might help you to find or reinforce yours, as I've learned from my teachers. This is how it seems to be working. I always recommend people read my books and watch films before making a decision to come to work with us. These are the invitation cards for a spiritual wedding, in which you can reunite with your deepest, truest self, the one you knew a long time ago, when you were a child. It is a relatively small investment of your time and money to ensure that a greater portion of it will be spent well.

If you resonate with my words, you will resonate with my medicine, for we are one. When you are free to leave your country and fly around the world again, I hope you feel the urgency of traveling to Peru to experience the medicine, since you never know when the window of opportunity will close up again. Recently, I passed the place where that archeological dig was happening and took a picture of the main square, which is empty. The most visited city in Peru looks dead. Who could ever have thought that Cusco would be empty of tourists?

Choosing to be worthy of your life and perhaps awaken to your purpose are the ingredients of spiritual healing. All you will be asked to sacrifice is your fear to be you, perhaps the deepest fear you have without knowing it, and something that you will find to be illusory as you move through it. A Huachuma experience is too deep for deception and too precious to doubt. It truly is what it is.

The Cactus of Sanity

FOOTNOTES

[1] https://www.amazon.com/-/es/Sergey-Baranov-ebook/dp/B00CMJCK6O/ref=sr_1_2?dchild=1&keywords=sergey+baranov&qid=1600448171&sr=8-2

[2] https://www.amazon.com/-/es/Sergey-Baranov-ebook/dp/B07G7DLXL3/ref=sr_1_1?_encoding=UTF8&dchild=1&qid=1601240662&refinements=p_27%3A+Sergey%5CcBaranov&s=digital-text&sr=1-1

[3] https://wakeup-world.com/2020/01/12/2020-a-year-of-chaos-and-great-opportunities/

[4] https://www.amazon.com/-/es/Sergey-Baranov/dp/1089247540/ref=sr_1_4?__mk_es_US=%C3%85M%C3%85%C5%BD%C3%95%C3%91&dchild=1&keywords=write+your+zen+in+30+days+sergey+baranov&qid=1600448407&sr=8-4

[5] http://news.unchealthcare.org/news/2020/june/roth-leads-26-9-million-project-to-create-better-psychiatric-medications

[6] https://www.thelancet.com/journals/lanpsy/article/PIIS2215-0366(16)30065-7/fulltext

[7] https://www.accessdata.fda.gov/drugsatfda_docs/label/2009/018936s075s077lbl.pdf

[8] https://www.darpa.mil/news-events/2019-09-11

[9] https://www.thelancet.com/journals/lanpsy/article/PIIS2215-0366(16)30065-7/fulltext

[10] https://www.thepharmaletter.com/article/are-big-pharma-and-big-tech-on-a-collision-course

[11] https://www.pewresearch.org/fact-tank/2014/01/02/more-than-half-of-cell-owners-affected-by-distracted-walking/

[12] https://www.researchgate.net/publication/236638569_Pedestrian_injuries_due_to_mobile_phone_use_in_public_places

[13] https://www.researchgate.net/publication/338526699_Selfie-death_and_its_implications_to_Mental_health_professionals

[14] https://variety.com/2018/digital/news/smartphone-addiction-study-check-phones-52-times-daily-1203028454/

[15] https://wakeup-world.com/2019/10/17/is-cannibalism-the-solution-to-food-sustainability-in-the-future/

[16] https://www.wired.com/2000/04/joy-2/

[17] https://pdfs.semanticscholar.org/2bbd/122436b9446a34cab84cb283d717bfa90e58.pdf?_ga=2.197467567.169600391.1597568728-543482055.1597568728

[18] https://www.edge.org/3rd_culture/ramachandran/ramachandran_index.html

[19] http://www.acad.bg/ebook/ml/Society of Mind.pdf

[20] https://www.youtube.com/watch?v=_bN4spt3744

The Cactus of Sanity

[21] http://www.psychedelic-library.org/peyote.htm
[22] https://www.youtube.com/watch?v=r4wQsmAtZoc
[23] https://www.youtube.com/watch?v=esPRsT-lmw8

Printed in Great Britain
by Amazon